my wife said

you may want

to marry me

"Jason B. Rosenthal's brilliant and achingly honest memoir
captures the true boundlessness of love and the absolute
heartbreak of loss. I smiled and cried the whole way through
this extraordinary reading experience, convinced more than
ever that, as Jason writes, 'people are good.'"

—John Green, #1 *New York Times* bestselling author of
Looking for Alaska and *The Fault in Our Stars*

"The book is a 228-page love declaration to Amy."

—*Washington Post*

"Rosenthal's grief journey is expressed with candor, humor,
and gratitude. . . . Recommended for readers either experiencing grief or wanting to understand how to support someone experiencing loss."

—*Library Journal*

"Jason's profoundly personal book is about loss and what
comes after, but it is, at its core, also the story of two soul
mates and a love that lives forever."

—Katie Couric, journalist,
New York Times bestselling author, and cancer advocate

my wife said
you may want
to marry me

a memoir

JASON B. ROSENTHAL

HARPER

NEW YORK ▪ LONDON ▪ TORONTO ▪ SYDNEY

HARPER

A hardcover edition of this book was published in 2020
by HarperCollins Publishers.

MY WIFE SAID YOU MAY WANT TO MARRY ME. Copyright © 2020 by
Jason B. Rosenthal. All rights reserved. Printed in the United States
of America. No part of this book may be used or reproduced in any
manner whatsoever without written permission except in the case of brief
quotations embodied in critical articles and reviews. For information,
address HarperCollins Publishers, 195 Broadway, New York, NY 10007.

You May Want to Marry My Husband first appeared in the *New
York Times* on March 3, 2017. © The New York Times Company.
Reprinted with permission.

My Wife Said You May Want to Marry Me first appeared in the *New
York Times* on June 15, 2018. © The New York Times Company.
Reprinted with permission.

*Illustrations by Brian Rea on pages 102 and 197
are used with permission of the artist.*

*Image on page 13 courtesy of Tom Lichtenheld. Images on pages 74, 81,
136, 175, 177, 184, 210, and 223 courtesy of Brooke Hummer.*

HarperCollins books may be purchased for educational, business, or
sales promotional use. For information, please email the Special Markets
Department at SPsales@harpercollins.com.

FIRST HARPER PAPERBACKS EDITION PUBLISHED 2021.

Library of Congress Cataloging-in-Publication Data has been applied for.

ISBN 978-0-06-294061-2 (pbk.)

21 22 23 24 25   LSC   10 9 8 7 6 5 4 3 2 1

Contents

Introduction

It is a tremendous act of violence to begin anything.
I am not able to begin. I simply skip what should be the beginning.

—*Rainer Maria Rilke*

I am writing this book because my wife died of ovarian cancer, but before you put it down and run in the other direction, please know, this won't be a maudlin tale of death.

It can't be.

The inspiration for writing this is a creative force, a woman who devoted her life to family, community, and connection, and had the kind of spirit we need a lot more of. She would have hated merely a dark tale of the end of life, because we had such a rich life together for over twenty-six years. Amy was an original. The last thing she would want is for the story of our lives together to wallow in humorless self-pity, because honestly, our time together had everything *but* that.

What this book is, instead, is an exploration of what it means to love, to lose, and to emerge from that loss somehow ready to be resilient in surprising and unexpected ways. It is a story of love and loss but also of appreciating the joy, beauty, and vitality of life. A story of how you come to the end of one part of your life and find a way to turn the page to the next. A story of my life with an exceptional woman, my wife, Amy Krouse Rosenthal. And a story of life without her as well.

Amy was an author, speaker, and filmmaker. As an author of two groundbreaking memoirs and as a children's book author, she has touched thousands of minds, both young and old, but the piece of writing she is best known for is an essay that appeared in the Modern Love column of the *New York Times*. It's called "You May Want to Marry My Husband," and it was published on March 3, 2017.

Ten days later, Amy died.

She was too ill to appreciate the response, but it was spectacular. Her essay immediately went viral and was ultimately read by more than five million people. The genuineness of her voice leapt off the page to all who encountered it. The article was many things, but most of all it was a message to me. In retrospect, I now think that Amy, who after all knew me better than any human on this planet after twenty-six years of marriage and building a family and life together, perhaps thought that I needed her express permission to find love after she died. It's a difficult thing for a dying spouse to say to her partner, let alone share with the entire world. And yet, like so much that Amy did, she pulled it off in a seemingly effortless manner.

The ten days between the date the essay was published and the day Amy died seemed like a microcosm of everything life has to offer—what should have been her highest high was tragically overshadowed by her imminent death. That impossible set of circumstances sent me on a journey I never imagined, didn't want, and couldn't have predicted; in one way it had an ending that came too soon. In another, it is an adventure that I will be on for the rest of my life. An odyssey that was made possible because of Amy.

In the years since Amy's death, I have spoken publicly about her quite a bit. I have talked about us together, and even about our family. I have tried to address people's astonishment at how we loved and understood each other so deeply. I have opened up about my personal experience with the issues of being with someone you love at the end of their life and of loss in general. I have also used the metaphor of the "empty space" that Amy gave me in her article to talk about resilience in the face of devastating loss. I have discussed the struggles of being single, single parenting, and doing something meaningful in my professional life while trying to fulfill her final wishes for me. However, I have not talked much about myself personally until now.

What follows in these pages is my attempt to share whatever small pieces of wisdom I've gained from an otherwise devastating process. Amy was a lot of things, but perhaps above all else, she was an optimist, her hunger for life insatiable. Her way of looking at the world was inspiring, even during difficult moments, and she would have delighted in the idea that some part of our story together could help someone else through their own personal darkness.

Not all love stories end the way you want them to, but often, that's what makes them worth telling.

PART I

The Nest

1

A Love Story

So, darling, be home soon
I couldn't bear to wait an extra minute if you dawdled
My darling, be home soon
It's not just these few hours, but I've been waiting since I toddled
For the great relief of having you to talk to.

—*John Sebastian*

I'm a Chicago guy, born and raised. And in order to understand where Amy and I began, it helps to understand where I began.

Family has always been the center of who I am. My parents divorced when I was two years old. For the next eight years, until my mom, Jo, remarried, it was just Mom; my older sister, Michel; and me. The way my mom raised me on her own established the core of the man I've become. She struggled and did her best, and she went back to grad school and got her master's degree in social work by the time I was five. (She's still practicing.) She was super liberal, always encouraging me to be independent and do my own thing, as long as "my own thing" wasn't stupid enough to throw my life out of order. I pushed the limits a little every once in a while, but I always respected her too much to make her wonder where I was or what I was doing.

My dad, Arnie, was a complicated man. He was definitely

around on occasional weekdays and weekend sleepovers, and this was one cool, fun dude in my formative years. He was handsome, with a full head of hair, so no surprise that he always had a girlfriend. He was into sports and music, an idiot savant when it came to jazz. He was a beautiful artist who could draw anything, and an art historian who could spend hours in a museum.

Dad was obsessively devoted to his mother, my grandma Sara, and he routinely took my sister and me to visit her in Skokie, Illinois, a hub of the Jewish community that settled there after World War II. Her community, just outside of the Chicago city limits, was also the focus of a court battle brought by the National Socialist (Nazi) Party of America to have the right to march in this neighborhood where many Holocaust survivors lived. Grandma Sara was a widow. She lived in a small apartment filled with furniture that was covered entirely in plastic—God forbid an unsanitary tush should make actual contact with the upholstery. No matter what restaurant we went to, particularly if it had bread service, Grandma Sara would inevitably walk out with a purse full of freebies. I'm pretty sure I even saw salt and pepper shakers in there a time or two. Sundays at her place were mostly spent watching the Chicago Bears on TV while my sister entertained herself doing anything else.

For most of my childhood Dad was in the advertising business, which I thought was a very sexy job. He was a highly intelligent man, but unfortunately, he wasn't the best at business. When I was in high school, he opened a commercial film studio in Lincoln Park. It seemed to be the culmination of Arnie's dream. It was also the perfect storm of his self-image as an "artist" and his earnest attempt at being a successful businessman, which is to say it didn't last as long as he'd hoped. But I have fond memories of working for him one summer in high school. I was, among other things, a production assistant—or, more accurately, an assistant to an assistant, driving a massively large van, picking up directors from the airport, and doing whatever grunt work no one else wanted to do. The hours were long, with plenty of all-nighters, but I was excited to have a closer look at what my dad was up to, and I learned a lot about the value of hard work and making money.

I was ten years old when Mom married my stepdad, Todd. They're still married today. Todd taught me how to balance a checkbook and how to put together model cars and airplanes, and he encouraged me to study science and read more. Todd brought my mom love and stability. He brought an intellectual curiosity, a sharp sense of humor, and a paternal voice to me and Michel.

Looking back at Amy's and my marriage, it would be tempting to surmise that I had a model for what it meant to be in a healthy relationship, and even what it takes to make a marriage work. Insert sound of game-show buzzer here: wrong. I can't quite pinpoint how I was ready to enter my relationship with Amy when I did. I was a mere kid at twenty-six. Reflecting back on the question now, it occurs to me that it is probably a combination of many factors—watching 1970s sitcoms, seeing some of my friends' parents, being solid in my own skin, my youthful ignorance, and falling in love with Amy. Oh, and a lot of luck. When I met Amy's family, I subconsciously thought, "Wow, if Amy came from this much love and warmth, maybe we could create this too."

Before I met Amy, I was what I've come to call a serial monogamist, starting with my first girlfriend in eighth grade, then in high school, followed by a long relationship in college. That is as serious as you can get when marriage isn't even on your radar. My mom had modeled for me what it was to be kind to people. My sister did as well. Perhaps part of me did not want the contentiousness of what I saw my mom and dad go through as a divorced couple. Maybe, if I am being honest with myself, I did not want to be like my dad when it came to relationships and women. Part of it was that I was a calm, openhearted guy who saw that women were far superior to us dudes, and a hell of a lot of fun to be around.

All that is to say that even though I was not ready when I first met Amy (I just never thought this would happen in my twenties), the process of falling in love and getting close to someone was not foreign to me. We were lucky. We fell in love, and I was all in.

I was in my third year of law school in Chicago when I got a call from "Uncle John." I'd known him since I was a kid—he'd dated my mom in the 1970s, when she was single—and unbeknownst to me until that day, he was apparently a modern-day male yenta.

It seemed his childhood friend Paul Krouse had a daughter named Amy, an advertising copywriter who'd just moved back to Chicago from San Francisco. I was twenty-four years old and single. Amy was twenty-four years old and single. John had known her since she was a kid too, and he had a premonition that she and I would hit it off.

I was slammed, in the throes of studying for the Illinois bar exam, but as a favor to John, I took down Amy's phone number, called her, and asked her out.

Our first date, the first and only blind date of my life, was on July 2, 1989.

I picked Amy up in my VW Golf (manual transmission, stick

shift). My first impressions were that she was super cute, tiny, full of energy, and immediately easy to talk to. She had long brown hair, not thick, that went beyond her shoulders. Dinner was at Jimmy and Johnnie's, an Italian restaurant that no longer exists. I remember almost everything about that dinner, from the food to the atmosphere to the company to the fact that Chicago Cubs first baseman Mark Grace was there, a few tables away. Then it was on to B.L.U.E.S., an intimate live blues music venue on Halsted Street.

It was a pretty special evening. Amy wrote, much later, that she knew she wanted to marry me by the time we finished eating. I knew I wanted to marry her a year later.

In many ways that summer was not an ideal time for me to start a relationship. I was preoccupied with my studies and lived almost every waking moment in the school's law library. Standardized tests in general are not my jam. Or, to put it another way, I'm not good at them at all. I knew that I had to devote most of my time to getting ready for this test.

But from that first date, I knew that Amy was too good not to prioritize. So in spite of my workload, Amy and I stayed in

How I still have my original note of Amy's phone number,
I have no idea, but here it is, misspelled last name and all.

touch and saw one another quite a few times. I'd never met anyone like her. It turned out she wasn't just super cute, tiny, full of energy, and easy to talk to. She was also smart, revealed a curiosity about pretty much everything, and possessed a contagious passion for life.

I remember our first kiss. We had been out on a bunch of dates throughout the summer and into the fall. I was living in a microscopic studio apartment near school, in Chicago's South Loop. The apartment was very small, like Amy herself. The kitchen was Manhattan size. My futon bed lived under the table in the main room. That's where I slept, *under* that table. The wall was covered with a huge chart I'd written out of the rule against perpetuities, an obscure probate precedent that I had to learn for the bar exam, with absurd phrases like "fertile octogenarian" and "unborn widow."

Amy and her ever-present brown backpack had come to visit. This wasn't just any backpack. This thing had a history. She'd

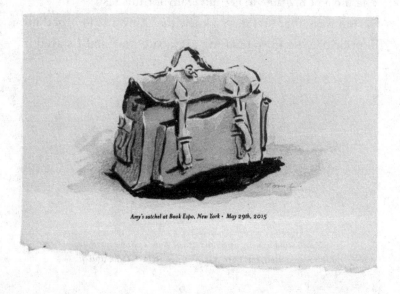

Amy's satchel at Book Expo, New York · May 29th, 2015

bought it in Greece during her college semester abroad, and you knew it had stories to tell. (It collected a lot more of them, since she kept right on carrying it for the next twenty-seven years.)

When the time came for her to leave, she slung the backpack over her shoulder, and I walked her to the door. As we stood in the open doorway, I moved in to kiss her, during which that big old bag slid off her shoulder and crashed, yanking her whole arm down with it.

It didn't stop us.

I'd planned a trip to celebrate the bar exam being mercifully over with. I was going to get in my VW and drive to the East Coast—first to Washington, DC, where I went to college; on to the Cape and Martha's Vineyard, where I had some friends; and then on to Boston and Buffalo. The trip lasted a few weeks. At this point, it felt like Amy and I were on solid footing in the relationship. Perhaps part of what brought clarity was the separation, my time to reflect on what was happening between us. I wanted her in my life, but thoughts of marriage, etc., were not in my mind. Amy and I corresponded during my trip. Good old-fashioned handwritten letters.

What is it about letters? Is it just the knowledge that physically putting a writing instrument to a piece of paper is a deliberate act, a gesture that requires forethought, and some intentional planning? Am I just old-fashioned? The more we communicate these days without writing at all—emojis, for example, and an endless stream of mystifying acronyms—the more meaningful the process of actually sitting down and writing a letter feels to me. Even emails, which now have algorithmic automatic response mechanisms, are hastily, carelessly written and sent, grammatical errors be damned.

a wonderfully delicious dinner at
Terczak's (the place on Halsted I
told you about) which not only filled me
to the gill but also provided leftover
which will serve rather nicely as a
dinner later this week. That place was
really good. My whole family went
plus my little sister's boyfriend (of
2 weeks) and my brother's girlfriend
(of 4 years!) — we laughed for
about 2 hours straight. About what?
I don't know but those other people
at the restaurant musta thought we
were loony (they're right) It would
have been fun having you there —
I think you'd have felt right at home
in the middle of all the craziness!
I do recall at one point laughing
hysterically about my mom's
mega-huge shoulder pads. All of
a sudden I just noticed how

Writing letters to Amy felt good, as if I was sharing my world with her in a literal and emotional way. And receiving letters from her was exciting on several levels, from the anticipation of opening the mailbox to the sight of her handwriting to the joy of sitting down to soak up her words.

An excerpt from a letter entitled "Monday," for example:

I am thinking about you. Kind of a lot. (How can I not with
Raphael perched on top of my computer?!) Love, Amy R. Krouse.

(Raphael, by the way, was the Teenage Mutant Ninja Turtle
I'd given her, for some reason I can't begin to remember.)
Or this very typical AKR passage:

We've got other things to chat about. What, I don't know. But
there's got to be something. Birds. Apples. Tennis. Hiccups.
Lima beans. Gladiators. Free association. It's bound to lead
to something. Porcupines. Nuts. Bambi. Tolstoy! That's it. Ya.
Tolstoy. Great guy, Tolstoy. A bit verbose though. Ya, forget him.
O.K. Pizza. Pencils. Key chain. How glad I am you're in my life.
Door knob. Fog.

With all this correspondence, I had an epiphany: I wanted
to bring Amy out to Cape Cod. After conspiring with her friend

Renee, I sent Amy eleven roses and a plane ticket. I enclosed a note in the box of flowers, telling her that the twelfth rose and I would be waiting for her when she arrived at the airport in Boston.

Mission accomplished. It was definitely a leap of faith for both of us. We didn't know each other that well, after all. But we both had a sense that something special was happening, and that visit to Cape Cod settled it for both of us.

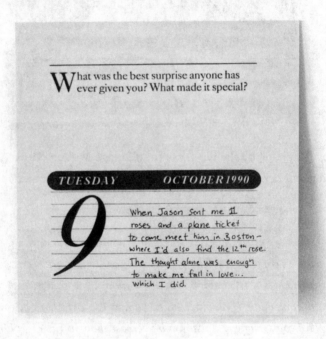

What was the best surprise anyone has ever given you? What made it special?

TUESDAY   OCTOBER 1990

9

When Jason sent me 11 roses and a plane ticket to come meet him in Boston — where I'd also find the 12th rose. The thought alone was enough to make me fall in love... which I did.

When I returned to Chicago, Amy and I dove deep into our relationship. We were so damned compatible. It was easy to be with this person. I talked to my mom, and she asked me to tell her what I liked about Amy. I remember answering, "Well, she's tiny, and we fit together so nicely."

That was certainly true. But the long answer was that she was a strong, independent woman. She was crazy smart and funny. Her smile was so infectious that it drew people to her, including me, obviously. She had lifelong friends. She was focused on her career. She loved music, art, and reading. She was devoted to her family, and they were so close to one another. And eventually I met that family.

I already felt as if I'd found nirvana when I met Amy. The addition of the Krouse family was a bonus beyond my wildest imagination. Holy cow, what fantastic people. Her parents, Ann and Paul, were clearly a connected, loving couple, kind, devoted to their children, and immediately welcoming to me. Ann still enjoys telling the story of how she and Amy were taking a walk after Amy and I met, and Amy was so enthusiastic—okay, effusive—about meeting me that it made her folks more accepting of me. Amy's siblings, Beth, Katie, and Joe, are amazing and loving, to one another and to me. They would all agree that Amy, as the eldest child, set the tone and paved the way for their incredible childhoods and family life.

Ann and Paul were successful, self-made people who'd started their own business and worked together every day of their lives for decades, so I guess it was kind of a natural evolution that as we began to spend more and more time together, Amy and I entered into the first of our two start-ups. Ready? A button business.

We scoured flea markets everywhere we went and snatched up any and all buttons that caught our eyes. Then, once we'd amassed a huge stash of an unbelievable variety of buttons, we began turning them into jewelry, mostly bracelets and brooches.

I'd never really pictured myself designing bracelets and brooches, but I have to say, there was something hypnotically mindful about the act of sewing buttons onto material. I even learned what "fray check" is (a liquid-plastic solution that stays invisible to give garments clean, perfect edges). The term *fray check* outlasted our button business—for years to come, one or the other of us would slip it into a conversation out of nowhere, and it made us laugh every single time.

Laughing together. Working together. Just being together. We had so much fun making, marketing, and selling our art. Somehow, without trying, this diminutive woman had filled me up with something I did not know I wanted or needed. I had not had it on my radar to commit to someone for the rest of my life at such a young age, but the natural way this relationship was developing felt just right.

Nothing
(For Jason)

There they were.
Limbs intertwined.
A human squiggle.
They thought about getting up to eat, it was probably time--
But they didn't.
They thought about turning on some music, the tv--
Why bother.
They thought maybe they'd go outside, take a walk--
But that didn't seem right either.
You have to understand that where they were
Was perfect.
There.
Together.
Still, they thought really they should get up and do something, anything.
But nothing was as good.
Nothing was as whole.
Nothing
Even came close.

March 1990

Then again, we began to enjoy our union no matter what we were doing together.

2

No Longer Just One

> I truly believe Jason loves you for exactly who you are, and that is what
> I prayed for you—for you to have someone who could appreciate and
> treasure all the wonderful facets of Amy.
>
> —Ann Wolk Krouse to her daughter Amy

Amy and I met in July 1989, and by November 1990 we were engaged. Of course, Amy would pick up on the acrostic nature of that coincidence: July, August, September, October, and November = **JASON**. Throughout that period, our feelings for each other grew in what felt to me to be a natural progression of a healthy relationship. I suppose I always knew I wanted to get married and have a family, but that was a concept I figured would come much later, or at least sometime after I turned thirty. With Amy, that simply was not meant to be. Our love grew as we spent more and more time together.

Consistent with what I imagined a quality young man was "supposed" to do, I asked Amy's folks for her hand in marriage. I went the traditional route—I bought a beautiful bouquet of flowers and a nice bottle of scotch before making the twenty-six-mile drive down the Edens Expressway to the Krouse house. Ann and Paul greeted me with their typical enthusiasm, and I nonchalantly strolled through their front door as if my arms weren't full of anything at all, let alone flowers and a fine scotch. They played along and didn't mention them either.

We took the long walk down to the family sunroom. I sat on the couch facing them, comfortable as always, and for about forty-five minutes, we just talked. Finally I presented the gifts, broached the subject at hand (pun intended), and told them why I was there. I promised them I'd love and respect Amy for the rest of my life. They didn't doubt it for a second, and gave me their delighted consent.

Around this time, my dad still owned his commercial film studio. I had my own set of keys, because I'd worked there. Having access to the studio allowed me to have epic high school parties there. (Sorry we never talked about that, Dad.) With some creative adjustments, it seemed like a perfect space for a marriage proposal.

Amy and I both had connections to Paris, France. My grandma Sara was born and raised there until she was thirteen years old. Amy was a French major and spent her junior year of college studying there. So I transformed the film stage into a replica of Paris and added a table with a red gingham tablecloth, complete with a bottle of wine, a candle, photos of the City of Romance, and a bread basket with the engagement ring hidden inside.

French music was playing in the background when I proposed.

She said yes.

Of course, there were no cell phones, so I borrowed a studio Polaroid camera, and am in possession of one photo memorializing the occasion.

We made it clear that we wanted a small wedding. Amy's

We met in July 1989. By November 1990, we were engaged.

(July, August, September, October, November.)

folks were a little disappointed—they'd been looking forward to celebrating the marriage of their eldest child with their vast group of friends.

We compromised and agreed to throw a big engagement party . . . our way. We rented a nice, spacious loft so there would be plenty of room for our guests. The loft happened to be in Chicago's South Loop, which in 1990 was an "emerging neighborhood," a polite way of saying it was in the early stages of gentrification but still kind of rough around the edges. The Krouses still chuckle to this day, looking back on the sight of 120 people in formal wear, many of whom were fresh from the safe, cozy suburbs, emerging from their cars and gaping around at a strange part of town for which they were decidedly overdressed.

Our wedding was as intimate and magical as we'd hoped. We held it at Amy's parents' home, which by definition guaranteed perfection, thanks to Ann's gifted attention to detail and planning. The gathering of Krouses and Rosenthals permeated the house with an almost palpable aura of love and family. My best friend Dave was my best man. He and I shared a scotch, in one of the Krouse kids' bedrooms that hadn't been redecorated since high school, while we got dressed for the evening's main event.

The ceremony went along beautifully and predictably until it was my turn to say my vows. No one was more surprised than I was when I suddenly burst into tears and began to weep like a baby. I'm still not sure exactly why.

Maybe I got hit by the colossal size of the commitment I was making at the ripe old age of twenty-six.

Maybe my tendency to bottle up my emotions and very rarely cry finally caught up with me.

Or, likeliest of all, maybe, standing there looking into my

bride's eyes, it hit me to my core that I was experiencing the most complete, most genuinely happy moment of my life.

Our honeymoon was perfect. We split the time between California and Colorado. In California we drove down Highway 1 along the Pacific coastline. We spent beautiful evenings at Ventana in Big Sur, a luxury hotel "where the sky, sea, mountains and redwoods all converge" (as they describe it on their website), and more beautiful evenings at the San Ysidro Ranch in the Santa Barbara foothills, overlooking the ocean. Colorado was a skiing excursion, during which I managed to dislocate my shoulder—again—but that did not alter my pure elation at the occasion or let it stop me, or us, for a second.

We were young, "deeply in love" is an understatement, and we were ecstatically excited about the infinite possibilities of the life we were starting together.

I got my first glimpse into living with a writer; when our conversation turned to thoughts about our future, we literally wrote out a list of our mutual marital commitments and gave it a title: "Amy and Jason Rosenthal's Marriage Goals and Ideas."

They were lofty intentions, but we lived by them—for the most part. We didn't do too well on the "lunch together once a week" thing, for example, because, well, life. In general, though, that simple list became the model we followed in our marriage. It established the foundation for how we wanted to be as people and as a couple as we began to start a family.

It made sense that it was formalized into a written list, too. For one thing, Amy was the queen of list-making, which she elevated into an art form. The idea of lists in general became ingrained in our family life. Yes, Amy was a list maker in all facets of her life, but the skill drifted in to all of our lives as well. There were lists for the babysitter, lists for how to spend the afternoon, lists analyzing a decision (pros and cons), and lists for me when Amy went out of town on a business trip.

Amy and Jason Rosenthal's
Marriage Goals and Ideas

1. Have lunch together at least once a week.

2. Keep sex fun.

3. Reading>TV.

4. Dinner time = time2B2gether. Music in the background is fine, TV is not.

5. Never stop learning! Take classes, read, cook and travel.

6. Get dressed up and go on dates.

7. Whenever we sign something "Amy & Jason," we both sign our name.

8. Annual portraits—"unadorned face" Start July, 1991, 25 years later (July, 2016) publish book! Entitled "Metamorphosis."

9. Record our kids' voices every year.

10. To, at some point (hopefully soon), work together, have our own business. Life is too short and we love being together too much to spend 9-5 apart every day.

11. Keep our cupboards & fridge continually stocked with good, healthy food.

For another thing, I'm not a neuropsychologist, but it's common sense to me that writing something down makes it more likely that you'll get it done, and that's what happened with this list. That list of marriage goals wasn't affixed to our nightstand or taped to the mirror in our bathroom—in fact I hadn't seen it for years until I came across it after Amy's death. But the muscle memory behind the emotions of the list had been powerful. We'd made it twenty-six years earlier, yet when I visited it again after so much time had passed, it felt so familiar. The specifics of this list we wrote on our honeymoon were recognizable for the way it guided our lives without staring us in the face. Without our realizing it, year after year it really did set the tone for addressing issues that came up during the course of our marriage. It set out our shared values when we were so young, and then those values manifested themselves without our trying to model them intentionally.

This thinking proved crucial early on in our marriage when we came to a crossroads, the biggest test we'd faced in our young lives together.

Amy was an established rock star in the advertising business by then. She was a copywriter, and she loved it. She'd come home with stories of what she and her colleagues did that day at work, and it sounded more like play to me. I'd never heard of a job like it. (My dad and stepdad were both in advertising but they never described their careers in this way!) She was a witty, smart, masterfully creative woman who thrived in the company of other witty, smart, masterfully creative people. She had a great reputation in the business, so it made perfect sense when one of the most sought-after firms in the country reached out to her with a job offer.

It was an incredible, well-deserved compliment, and an amazing opportunity. Amy was as giddy as a little girl, and I couldn't have been happier for her. There was just one downside: The job would require us to move to Portland, Oregon. Two thousand miles from home. We had no family in Portland, and maybe one friend.

I was just beginning to establish myself as a Chicago lawyer. Though I was working at a small firm, I had dreamed of opening my own practice as a solo practitioner instead of joining a firm. The dream to hang out my own shingle came from my life as an entrepreneur. From an early age I'd held a job. This process began when I was eight years old and had my own paper route. From there, I worked steadily all through law school in different fields. Also, my role modeling for a career path up to this point came from my parents, who were both self-employed their entire adult lives. And all of my contacts were in my hometown. If I was going to build a business, the odds were in favor of my building it there.

At the same time, though, I was excited for Amy's opportunity to soar in a career in which she was already a heavyweight and work on some of the most creative campaigns in the country.

So we took a trip to Portland. Amy interviewed with the ad agency, while I had a few informal chats with a couple of law firms and the legal department at the Nike campus. Nice people. Nice city. Great potential. No red flags.

Next we sat down with Ann and Paul, Amy's parents, whose advice we'd always respected. We met them for lunch, and Amy launched into a detailed description of this incredible job offer from this prestigious company. Okay, Portland, but she was so excited as she told them about it that she could barely contain herself.

Their response was immediate and definitive—incredulous,

they threw down the gauntlet. How could Amy be so selfish? What about me and my fledgling career? What about the fact that saying yes to this job offer would mean a two-thousand-mile separation between us and our families, all of whom lived right here in the area? Yes, it was a prestigious offer, but that only made it even more likely that she could find something equally prestigious in Chicago, or at least a whole lot closer to home.

I'd never seen Amy cry so hard in our newly formed bond. She was so emotionally fraught, wanting so badly to fulfill this dream but knowing that the practicality of her parents' advice was spot-on. Our final decision was arrived at through many tears and conversations; we practiced our list-making prowess, wrote out the pros and cons on paper, and took a deep dive into what the consequences of staying home meant for both of our careers.

In the end, we chose Chicago. We chose home. We chose family.

And we grew, individually and as a couple, from the whole experience.

We never looked back, and one by one we checked off marriage goals and ideas to help keep us moving forward.

Keep sex fun. No problem there. End of discussion.

Reading>TV. We deliberately never, ever had a TV in our bedroom. Amy's nightstand was always stacked with the books she devoured. I read every night too; but unlike Amy, I was always out cold after a couple of paragraphs. I'd invariably wake up sometime during the night with the book perched on my chest, still held in my hands. Years later, when my insomnia kicked in, I developed the habit of waking up, climbing out of bed with my book, and settling in to read in the barber chair I kept in the corner of our bedroom until fatigue finally kicked in.

Whenever we sign something "Amy & Jason," we both sign our name. Absolutely. Literally every single time.

To, at some point (hopefully soon), work together, have our own business. Life is too short and we love being together too much to spend 9–5 apart every day. The nine-to-five thing wasn't very realistic, it turned out, with both of us hard at work on our full-time careers. But spurred on by how much we'd enjoyed our button business, we plunged headlong into a sideline T-shirt business under the banner of 272 Productions, a blend of Amy's childhood phone number and an homage to July 2 (7/2), the night of our first date.

For the most part, Amy was our one-woman creative department, while I was in charge of marketing, operations, and legal. Some of the designs were originals. We licensed others from artists and writers. We worked hard at it, and we loved it. There

were the "Tee for Two" T-shirts, sold as a pair, each bearing half of the yin/yang symbol. There were such favorites as "Does 'anal retentive' have a hyphen?"; "I'd love to have a nervous breakdown but I can't seem to find the time"; "procrastinate later"; and "Just because I have a short attention span doesn't mean I."

When the Chicago Bulls won their first three championships, we came up with the design of three images of Peter Brady from *The Brady Bunch* and the caption "3 Pete," a wordplay on the popular term *three-peat*, for when a team wins three championships in a row. Brilliant, right? Unfortunately, we couldn't get the requisite licensing, so those T-shirts are still sitting in mothballs.

We had such a great time, and overall sales were going so well that more than once I was tempted to give up my day job, but I never quite managed to pull the trigger.

And then there was "**Never stop learning! Take classes, read, cook, and travel.**" Oh, yes. We lived by this big-time.

Amy's art director at the ad agency became a close friend. The two women worked long, intense days together, even longer and more intense than my days as a young lawyer. It grew into a tradition for us to meet after work at the art director's house, around nine p.m., for copious amounts of French red wine and a spectacular meal prepared by her husband, Tom, who happened to be a gourmet chef.

For my twenty-fifth birthday, Amy gave me a brilliant gift she knew she'd end up enjoying as much as I would—a series of cooking lessons from Tom. The routine went like this: I'd head to Tom's after work. He'd already have a meal designed to teach me. We'd discuss it over a preparatory scotch and then start cooking. By the time our wives got home from work, we'd have a feast waiting for them, along with an appropriately breathed bottle of wine.

Thanks to Tom, and Amy's flair for creative gift-giving, I learned how to make everything from bechamel sauce to tapenade to fish prepared according to the Canadian cooking method. Perhaps Amy knew, even this early in our relationship, that my creativity was deep-rooted. She was prescient, anticipating that my day job as a lawyer would always be a struggle for me.

And still on the subject of "Never stop learning!," Amy also encouraged me to follow through on the desire I had always had to paint. I had never studied art. The closest I had ever come was a woodshop class in grade school, in the basement of a Chicago Park District building. (I can still smell the burning wood as I write this.) I learned how to use a table saw and made a shelf my father hung in his groovy apartment in the 1970s. I might have made a lamp as well. But the instructor never implied that I should consider turning pro at woodworking, and it didn't really satisfy the "artist" part of me that I probably inherited from Dad.

I signed up for classes in the studio of an accomplished professional painter. It was me and three or four other students, depending on the week, all women of retirement age; and it was, in a word, fabulous. I learned the color wheel. I learned to love mixing colors, making beautiful grays from various combinations of blue and orange and differing amounts of white. I learned how to put together an abstract acrylic painting. I learned that I love the hypnotic act of painting, and the solitude and focus of it. I learned that I love to create.

I've never been sure if my paintings are any good. All I was sure of, all that mattered, was that Amy was a huge, enthusiastic

fan. In fact, a part of her wanted me to paint on a more regular basis, maybe tip the scale more toward my artwork and away from my nine-to-five job as a lawyer. Again, I never could bring myself to pull that trigger; but just knowing she believed in me that much has kept me painting to this very day.

We also became regular practitioners of ashtanga yoga, a very intense form of practice. For a while we had an instructor, Lisa, come to our house to help me get familiar with the intricacies of the practice. Even after more than a decade, I never gained much flexibility in my stiff hips, while Amy was Gumby-like from the very beginning. I did have the distinction, though, of being Lisa's only student who practiced to the music of Nine Inch Nails. Yoga grew to be a huge part of our lives, and when time and life allowed, we traveled the world together, seeking out yoga destinations. (Subgoal no. 4 of **Never stop learning!: travel**.)

Many years later we started frequenting a historic place

called the Green Mill on Broadway in uptown Chicago. It's the oldest jazz club in the United States, and apparently it was a favorite haunt of Al Capone's. Of infinitely more interest to us was the fact that Thursday nights at the Green Mill showcased the most exquisite professional and amateur dancers of all ages. There they'd be, effortless and intoxicating, swing dancing on a tiny dance floor in front of a big band, surrounded by tables of patrons sipping martinis.

It didn't take long for us to decide that as much fun as it was to watch, it would probably be even more fun to do. We managed to track down a teacher who'd taught many of those Green Mill dancers and hired her to give us private swing/big band dance lessons. We were so excited.

Unfortunately, as life would have it, we had to quit after just one class.

But I'm getting way ahead of myself.

Looking back on that list, so many of the things on it would later define our marriage. Even something as simple as my skills in the kitchen. The seeds of the strength of our marriage were in that list. So much of what we were and what we became was possible because of that list.

We were doing pretty well so far with our marriage goals and ideas, but there was one item we couldn't possibly accomplish on our own—and we were determined to do something about it.

After all, how were we supposed to **record our kids' voices every year** if we didn't have kids?

3

Fun, Whimsical, and Creative Parenting

Between the artwork plastering the walls, and the magnet that read "Our house is clean enough to be healthy and messy enough to be happy," there was an element of contentedness in your household that made it happy and secure.

—*Nadia Razaq Sutton, a former babysitter*

Raising a family with Amy was the greatest adventure of my life. Boy, is that a huge understatement.

I've never had any complaints about my childhood, but I suppose on paper it might qualify as a bit dysfunctional—my parents divorced when I was two. My mother exhibited masterful parenting skills while raising my sister and me as a single parent. During this time, my dad, too, was single and had lots of girlfriends. It was either because of that, or in spite of it, that by the time I was grown-up (relatively speaking) and married to Amy, family had become incredibly important to me. In fact, one of the thousands of reasons Amy's dad became one of my heroes is that he was the patriarch of his family, which eventually grew to twenty-three of us; and he never, ever passed up an opportunity, in conversations or behavior in general, to make it clear that family *always* came first for him and my mother-in-law.

So when, on our second wedding anniversary, we brought home our firstborn son, I was the happiest man on earth.

Justin was a chubby, blue-eyed beauty who entered the world with the personality he still maintains today. We were in awe of him, and not long after he was born, rather than be held down by his arrival, we simply made him our companion everywhere we went. We took him to restaurants, plopping him down in his car seat on a chair next to us and praying that he'd stay asleep while we ate. We took him on countless trips to spend time with the family, so he'd know from the time he was a baby that there was this whole group of people named Krouse and Rosenthal he was connected to, people who adored him and would always take care of him. They all marveled at this fascinating new little person, an extension of us and all of them; and without even trying he'd instantly transform them from perfectly articulate adults to a bunch of softies whose conversation was limited to gushing and baby noises.

Justin is brilliant. He always has been. From the moment he began to formulate and articulate thoughts, he blew us away with some of his perfunctory pronouncements, many of which Amy documented.

Justin, age eight: "When I graduate college, I'm getting in my car and going straight to see all the R-rated movies." And when Amy said to him, "You were my little baby, and now look at you. How did you get so big?" he replied, without missing a beat, "Mom, it's called life."

Sometimes he showed a poignancy and a depth way beyond his years. Justin, age nine: "Mom, if you were God, and someone killed someone, but spent the rest of their life rescuing people, taking in stray animals, picking up litter, and doing mitzvahs, would you put them in heaven or hell?"

I mean, seriously, with a mind like that, is it any wonder he was extremely comfortable in the company of adults from the moment he was born?

Less than two years later, our son Miles arrived. Sweet and thoughtful, he was a natural addition to the growing Rosenthal clan. Justin was instantly fascinated with his little brother, and in no time at all, the two of them became inseparable. They were more like big cat cubs, and they literally would have preferred to be. They were rough and funny and loud, with a few inevitable injuries here and there, but from the very beginning they were so close that this union of "the boys," as they became known, was solidified.

Miles has always been a combination of jock and philosopher. He stormed out of the womb a lithe, athletic boy, constantly running, jumping, and climbing the walls. He spent much of his childhood as Spider-Man, clinging to the highest point of every doorframe in the house. At the same time, he was a deep thinker who later became an avid reader. He was nine years old when he said, "I'm always thinking about something. And if I'm not thinking, then I'm writing words in my mind in cursive. Like I just wrote the word 'door.' "

He was also a talker, with a wild imagination. Want to hear what he dreamed last night? Get yourself some coffee and strap in—this is going to take a while. Miles was as endlessly entertaining as his brother, and Amy and I loved nothing more in this world than the daily wonder of getting to know our two precious sons.

When Amy got pregnant with our third child, we knew it would be another boy. I mean, we obviously made boys, so what else could it possibly be? The answer, of course, to our surprise and joy: a gorgeous blue-eyed baby girl, who emerged from the womb with a full head of dark hair. For reasons you already know from reading about the night I proposed to Amy, we named her Paris.

Paris had an immediate, profound connection to her mom, almost as if they'd known each other in a past life and were just thrilled to be reunited in this one. She was still very little when she told Amy one day, "I always get confused in the morning because you're always in my dreams, so I think you already know them."

As a tiny person, she was empathetic, which is a quality that has never left her. She was four years old when the horrifying tragedy of September 11, 2001, stunned us all. Paris took it upon herself to color American flags to sell so that she could donate the money to the victims' families. She was born with a soul-deep sense of family that's still reflected in the life she lives today, and she inherited her mother's uncanny flair for translating a list-making compulsion into a solid career as an author. (Her first lists, from the moment she was able to write, were simply the names of all our family members, including a whole lot of cousins, to whom our three kids have always been close.)

Of course, with three kids you would think that the entry from our marriage goals list that read **Record our kids' voices every year** would have been no sweat. Full disclosure: we failed miserably. I did manage to capture Justin's tiny voice as he navigated a golf cart on one of our family vacations. I recorded Miles, age four, reciting a story he'd somehow memorized from the tapes we played on trips in our minivan. And seven-year-old Paris was preserved by Amy in a home movie, giggling and being super silly after drawing eyes on her chin so that she still had a right-side-up face when she was upside down. But "every year" slipped through the cracks. I wish it hadn't.

There were other failures on that list as well. When it came to **Annual Portraits**—"unadorned face" . . . what a fabulous idea. You should do it! (Never happened.) In our defense, we did take "couch pictures" *almost* every year, kind of a spontaneous, come-as-you-are impulse. We'd plop down on the family room couch and take a picture in whatever we were wearing, funky hair and all, from the time the kids were tiny blobs until they'd sprouted up to be quite a bit taller than their mommy. Not exactly the annual portraits we might have had in mind on our honeymoon when we made the original list of goals, but definitely the style of the family we'd become.

I'm proud to say, though, that there were several other entries on that list at which we absolutely excelled, which became both more challenging and more important after kids.

Take, for example, **Get dressed up and go on dates**. Yes! Even when the kids were very little, Saturday night was date night for Amy and me. If I had it to do over, I'm not sure I'd still leave a thirteen-year-old girl in charge of three small children; but she was reliable, the kids liked her, and she seemed to enjoy it.

We'd begin with a yoga session in Amy's home office. Then we'd get showered and nicely dressed and leave instructions for the babysitter: "We picked out a VHS from Blockbuster. Here you go. Pizza's in the freezer. We won't be late."

It never really mattered where we went or what we did. Dinner and a martini at a local joint, typically sitting at the bar.

Out with friends. Music. Lots of live music. The point was being together, making time for each other, seeing to it that the noise of life, kids, work, whatever, didn't drown out the amazing "us" at the core of it all. Our weekly dates were the equivalent of recharging an electric vehicle, sitting for a good meditation, or taking a short vacation. They never became stale. In fact, somehow they always seemed to infuse new life into a relationship that was already thriving.

One of the spots we loved to return to on these dates was Millennium Park. Their programming was filled with contemporary music and world music on some nights and classical on others. We developed a routine of taking the CTA train to the park. But sometimes, since the park was close to my office, I would meet Amy there after work; she would walk the entire way from our house, an approximately two-hour journey. I think she could have kept going all the way to Indiana. I usually packed a picnic for us. Cheese, lots of cheese, an AKR favorite. A charcuterie assortment, fruit, and either a roadie martini or red wine. We also had an entire assembly of blankets, Crazy Creek chairs, and a snazzy backpack with plates and cups. This type of evening was so beautiful, taking in the Chicago skyline and the warm summer nights. It became "our spot" and the setting for many future Amy events.

Another favorite was a neighborhood joint called Katerina's. Katerina was a lovely woman who opened a coffee shop near our house. Amy spent many days there working on her writing and encountered quite a cast of characters over the years. Katerina always wanted to open a jazz club and have a liquor license. Eventually she managed to navigate the bureaucracy, obtain the appropriate licensing, and open a bar and jazz music venue. Amy and I spent frequent date nights enjoying Katerina's hospitality. We would sit at the bar and order a martini. Typically, as was not uncommon for Amy's thirst for all things, she would order one martini, quickly down it, and order another. One hundred percent of the time, she took a sip or two of the second and reached her limit. In all of our years together, in fact, I never saw her have more than two drinks. Katerina's was filled with good traditional Greek food and inspiring live music. It was a perfect date for us, combining many of our favorite things.

Keep our cupboards & fridge continually stocked with good, healthy food. Absolutely. With the exception of Amy's propensity toward mayonnaise and her infatuation with chips, we insisted on and modeled healthy eating for our kids. Believe me, we knew how fortunate we were to be able to provide those healthy options, too. Living in our divided city of Chicago, I've been exposed to all types of people; and I'm well aware that many families don't understand what healthy eating even means—parents were either never exposed to it in their lives or lived below the poverty line and thought they couldn't afford it. I've seen more than my share of kids walking to school drinking grape soda and reaching into bags of flamin' hot chips with their orange-stained fingers. That Amy and I had the backgrounds and education to raise our children knowing the importance of good nutrition and fill our cupboards and fridge accordingly, and that the message has stayed with them as they've begun to navigate the world as young adults, are things I've never taken for granted.

Dinner time = time2B2gether. Music in the background is fine, TV is not. Amy and I followed that rule religiously when it was just the two of us. It became even more ingrained in our family when it was the five of us. Throughout my professional life, I was able to work hard six days a week and still manage to be home every night for dinner. It was an invaluable daily chance for us to check in and stay current with each other, as individuals and as a family. It's amazing how freely information can flow when there's no agenda, nothing specific to talk about or serve as a "teaching moment." Sometimes the conversations would be intense. Sometimes they'd be trivial, just typical observations and events in the lives of working parents and the progressions of their children from grade school through high school. "Trivial" never meant "unimportant," though, so no one ever left the dinner feeling as if what they had to say didn't matter.

Mostly, though, our nightly dinners included a lot of laughter. Sometimes we were funny or silly together. And okay, we weren't above involuntarily laughing when someone let loose with an inappropriate bodily sound or decided to try out cursing as a possible new means of communication. The kids enjoyed those family dinners together as much as Amy and I did.

From time to time, as a reflection of the joyful, innately fun tone Amy set for her life and ours, we'd celebrate Backwards Night. The evening would start with bedtime stories, affectionately known as "yellows" in our house because some of the stories came from a yellow-covered book. This would transition into bath time, invariably a raucous exercise in silliness that included lions and tigers, Pokémon, and artwork on the chalkboard-painted wall around the tub. Next up was dessert, followed by our usual family dinner. This whimsical tradition is just one example of how parenting with Amy was such a joy.

Before the kids entered preschool, Amy and I agreed that

infusing their lives with Jewish culture was important to us. I'd attended a Jewish day school in Chicago. Amy? She and her dad would leave the house every week so that he could take her to Sunday school. More times than not he'd end up taking her out to eat instead. But despite our detachment from organized religion, we had great mutual respect for our cultural traditions and values and wanted them for our family. So we sent the children to a Jewish preschool, and then day school, where they learned some of those traditions and brought them home.

One that stuck, and became meaningful in so many ways, was our Friday-night Shabbat dinners. They were a time to enjoy not only each other but our extended family and our wider community as well. Many of the dinners were just us five "Rosies," as we were affectionately known. Sometimes family joined in. Other times, family friends and their kids came over, or we would go to their homes instead. Whatever the details, Shabbat dinners meant slowing down from a hectic week. They meant being together for traditional prayers, including a prayer Amy always recited specifically for the children. Candles were lit, wine was poured, and bread was broken. Simple. Quietly reverent. And always, always full of gratitude.

Before long we added a personal tradition to our Shabbat dinners that became a family favorite. Amy and I had a green letter *R* made of metal we'd acquired over the years, and we began passing the *R* among everyone who'd joined us at the table. Whoever ended up holding the *R* had to share a story from the previous week, some moment or event that had an emotional impact on them, good or bad. It was a little nerve-racking at first for those who were shy about opening up to a room full of people, but before long, because there was plenty of support and no judgment at that table, they began looking forward to passing the *R* at the Rosenthal Shabbat dinners. Many of our kids' friends, who are now young adults, still look back fondly on those wonderful Friday evenings. So do our kids. So do I. As much as I treasured them, I never stop appreciating how much richer they were because Justin, Miles, and Paris were part of them.

When it was time to revisit the travel part of **Never stop learning!**, there were two categories: family travel and separately, just the two of us.

Every summer Amy and I would set aside a month (I was self-employed, with a supertough boss, but stressful as it was to take the time off, it was also a no-brainer for me to join in for two of those weeks), and off the five of us would go, to destinations all over the world. One of the many stunning qualities about Amy that I have never encountered in any other person in my life was her commitment to follow through on issues big and small. So many of us have dreams about the way our lives should be lived. We talk about doing this and that "when we have time," or "when work slows down," or "when we have the finances in order." With Amy, if she set a goal to do something— professionally or personally—she made sure to follow through. I have encountered so many people who have regaled me with stories about working with Amy. She never hesitated to make her opinions known, and she knew just what she wanted. While this sometimes came across as intense, each and every story ended with Amy making the person better, and the experience they shared was priceless.

In our relationship, Amy also pushed me to follow through. For example, the mere thought of taking a month, *a month*, out of our lives to travel with our children took some serious getting used to for me. Don't get me wrong, it was something we talked about often, but putting it into practice was another thing altogether. Amy made it happen. Of course, once we made it to our destination of choice, the reasons for the trip, and its value to our family, became so clear—the exposure to different cultures, the chance to slow down, and most important, the time to be just us Rosies.

And whatever the destination, we Rosies weren't there to sightsee. We were there, wherever "there" happened to be, to soak up the culture of whatever location we chose to visit. Often this meant renting a place and living, truly engaging, with a specific community. We'd walk to local markets to shop, meet our "neighbors," and prepare our own meals. We'd spend time in the most populated parks or beaches and support the local vendors. If we were in Europe, we'd eat dinner at 9:00 p.m. like the locals. In Wyoming, we made peach cobbler over an open fire. In Italy, we picked the endemic rosemary, and our family friend there would help us use it to cook feasts. Justin made friends with an octogenarian neighbor at our place in Italy. He was enamored with her dog, but the two of them hit it off as well. He remained pen pals with that woman when we returned home.

Travel provided a great opportunity to teach our kids the value of making a difference through social service. We frequently found social service activities when we traveled the world. On occasion, we went to a specific destination purposefully to volunteer at a local organization. Amy and the kids traveled to Brazil to work in an orphanage and a preschool. We all went to Guatemala to build stoves out of brick and mortar for families who were so impoverished that they were literally cooking over open flames in their small shacks, routinely filling their living spaces with carcinogenic smoke.

We also went out of our way to create moments of boredom—healthy moments of doing nothing, just interacting with one another in ways that the pace of everyday life back home didn't allow. We colored. We played hide-and-seek. We played Uno, gin rummy, Scrabble, backgammon, and Mastermind. We specialized in family-made obstacle courses. And we kept growing closer and closer.

If you've never shared gratifying experiences like these with your children, I can't recommend it strongly enough. They bring out the best in all of you; they give you memories and a sense of giving back that will last a lifetime; they expose your children to other cultures and people whose lives they'll change with simple acts of kindness; and your family, like ours, will find yourselves even closer than you ever dreamed possible.

I know I've made this marriage and this family sound like a fantasy. Well, guess what—they pretty much were. There were certainly moments when our marriage was strained, but honestly, not too many.

There was a stretch of time when we had two kids in diapers for six years straight, and sleep deprivation didn't exactly bring out the best in either of us. We wrestled with whether to retrieve a crying child at bedtime or let them cry themselves to sleep and the pragmatic issues of three kids on three different schedules, none of which were always compatible with our own schedules. And then there was the inevitable debate that starts with "Your turn to put the kids down," followed by an incredulous "Wait, I put them down last time! I'm sure it's your turn."

There were also issues about time in general. Amy couldn't tolerate my being home even slightly later than I said I'd be. And I couldn't tolerate a habit of hers when we went to family gatherings, which usually went something like this:

Drive forty-five minutes to her parents' house. Spend the entire day with them, her siblings, and a flock of cousins, which invariably bled over into dinner. Start the forty-five-minute drive back to Chicago much later than planned, while the kids fall asleep in the minivan.

I was done, and then some, by the time we left. On more than one occasion, Amy wasn't—she'd suddenly get the bright idea that we should stop to visit a friend on the way home, wanting as usual to pack in as much fun as possible in a day, a week, a year, a life.

My invariable response: No. Just no. The end. Amy would understand and be okay with it. This was part of her wanting "more," her first word. Her dad often told this story, and it became part of the Krouse family lore.

Those fairly standard-issue difficulties, believe it or not, were pretty much the worst of the "problems" in our marriage, and we never let them escalate. We'd worked side by side in third-world countries, after all; we had a fairly healthy handle on where our problems ranked on a scale of one to destitute. But even more than that, we shared such an incredible alignment on the big issues that the small, inconsequential ones were all we had left to make noise about.

And then of course there were the worries I carried around. They were the kinds of concerns that most people have, but unfortunately their ubiquity doesn't make them any less potent, especially at two in the morning.

I've never been an especially good sleeper. What did I think about in the middle of the night, when my body was still and my mind was racing? I wish I could say I was thinking about how the man-made climate crisis would impact my children and grandchildren. Maybe I would be a better person if my thoughts had shifted to how to solve the gun crisis in Chicago and around the nation. But in reality, they often focused on whether a check would come in that month from my law practice. My chosen field, personal injury litigation, is a contingency-fee arrangement between lawyer and client. Of course, this means that the only way you get paid is if you settle or win the cases. This translates to a feast-or-famine lifestyle; some cases took years to resolve, others not so long.

Oh, and did I mention that I made a huge work transition when I had two kids in diapers and a mortgage? Yep. Amy was working for a large advertising firm and had health benefits, so I jumped on the opportunity to open my own firm. I know, great timing. But if I was going to do this, now was the time. Or is there ever a good time? So I took the leap. Surely the stress of this transition came into play as my sleep issues continued to intensify. In the morning those demons would disappear and I would put my head down and go to the office to do something about it, but that rationality does not surface when extreme fatigue is kicking in during the wee hours of the still night.

There were personal issues as well. Were my kids okay? There were some behavioral shifts. Was all of this normal? Additionally, there were the existential issues I was thinking about as I began to get older. What was I doing every day to make this world a better place? Was I doing enough social service work? Certainly I could spend more of my time volunteering right here in my own city. In my limited time on this planet, was I making a difference? Any impact at all?

Lying right next to me each night was Amy, sleeping soundly, averaging a solid eight hours without a peep. Not only that, but she got up in the morning, placed her tiny feet on the ground, and set off on her day. She had things to do. Ideas to put on paper or on film. Notes to write on her hand. Lists to make. Kids to embrace. Clearly, the energy she used every minute of every day made her hit the pillow hard at night—the only time her mind was *not* racing, in contrast to my own.

Amy never did cease to amaze me. By the time we had our third child, the sweet angel Paris, and Amy was on maternity leave from her advertising job, a profound feeling of motherhood swept over her, and we talked about her becoming a full-time writer. Without missing a beat at her full-time, well-paid advertising gig, she'd managed to write and publish two adult books in the category of nonfiction humor or observations about life from the unique AKR perspective. This was not an easy process. Amy herself displayed with pride her many, many rejection letters.

But her talent as a writer was undeniable, and as she mulled over trying her hand at it full-time, we both knew that, like my transition, there was no "good" time to do this. Our relationship was so solid, though, that we really supported each other in every way. I knew the change would not be easy financially, but we were okay. If this is what Amy wanted to do, I was behind her 100 percent. While her first books were not flying off the shelf, Amy had a huge idea for a memoir-style book, and she was jazzed about it. So she quit her advertising career and became an author.

It was not until we were navigating our second pairing of two kids in diapers that Amy had an epiphany: she would write a children's book. Paris was two years old. She was so verbal already, it was crazy. This was a popular question in our household at night: "Mommy, will you read me a story?" From this innocent, sweet question, Little Pea was "sprouted," as Amy told it. She was putting Paris to bed, closing her eyes as she usually had to do for inspiration when she told the kids a story. The bedtime tale came flowing out that would ultimately be published as *Little Pea*, the tale of a pea who couldn't stomach the thought of eating candy, but couldn't wait for his favorite food—spinach.

Now, this is not the first time that Amy got the response, "Mom, that is the best story ever!" She described our kids as the best, most forgiving audience. But this was special, so she

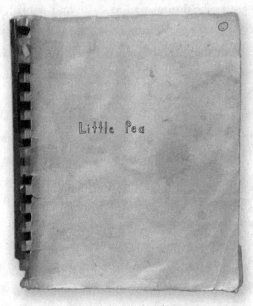

Original sketch of Little Pea.

wrote it down the next day. It was six years door-to-door for Mr. Pea, but he was published with stunning illustrations in 2005.

When Amy made the total transformation to full-time author, I was elated. She would go on to write, and have published, about thirty-five children's books in fourteen years, including her posthumous publications—an amazing clip.

While I certainly had my own demons about my work life, I could not have been happier for Amy. I never once made a comparison. Sure, I thought "How can someone be so happy and fulfilled *every day* of her work life?" I just did not think a lawyer could get to that place. Nor did I think any other people I'd known in my life had ever reached that pinnacle either. I think one of the main reasons our marriage worked so well was that we genuinely wanted each other to be happy, to succeed, to make an impact, and to find inspiration. We were there for one another always. Amy was quirky, some say nontraditional, but she was Amy, and I would never have wanted to change one single thing about her, despite her desire to be taller and have thicker hair.

Seeing Amy go through this transition in her professional life made it hard for me, though, as I struggled with ambivalence about my own vocation. For years I'd been struggling to find meaning in my law career. Sure, I had many moments of stimulation, some appreciative clients, and financial success. But much of my daily work was mired in the painfully slow judicial system, the impersonal shortsightedness of insurance companies, and some very *un*appreciative clients.

Hoping to revitalize my attitude toward my professional life, I took on real estate investing as a simultaneous second career; and I have to say it was actually exciting and fulfilling in a lot of ways that being a lawyer wasn't. I invested in value-added properties and some new construction, and I owned a bunch of residential buildings on the south and west sides of Chicago. I started to feel some glimmers of stimulation again, and I certainly met a lot of fascinating people and families I would never have met otherwise. One particular tenant I recall fondly used to set aside a plate just for me whenever she was making her specialties—chicken, collard greens, corn bread, and sweet potato pie. She was warm, lovely, and grateful. So were most of my tenants.

"Make the most of your time here" was one of Amy's mottos. She reminded anyone who would listen of that motto often, including me. If I was mired down in the minutiae of my law practice, she would suggest I go into my studio and paint. When I expressed enthusiasm for dabbling in the real estate game, and she saw my passion for it, she strongly encouraged me to give it a shot. If one of my favorite bands was in town, and it was a dude show she would not be interested in, she would encourage me to go with friends. I never played golf when the kids were young, knowing how much time it would take away from our family life. However, when her dad and her brother talked up how much fun it was, she fully endorsed my foray into the sport. In everyday life she did the same, whether it was complimenting me on an outfit—"Oh, you look so cute," admiring a toast I had given at one of our dinner parties, or, after reading one of my many cards to her, saying that I was the writer in the family, "really." She made me a better person, through her actions and her words. And as I look back, I am pretty sure I did the same for her.

4

On Our Own

I wanted to know each part
Want to know each part of you

—*Andy Hull, Manchester Orchestra*

And then one day in 2015, after twenty-four years of barreling forward hand in hand through three kids, diapers, good teachers, laughing through family dinners, scraped knees, soccer practices, report cards, school pictures, bad teachers, college essays, date-night martinis, and all the rest, impossibly, we started making plans for the fact that we were about to become empty-nesters.

Justin was living in Texas, starting his adult work life while continuing to pursue his degree.

Miles was in college in Atlanta.

Paris had been in Canada for the summer, preparing for her upcoming soccer season, before starting her freshman year in college in September.

For so many years that reality had seemed like a lifetime away. When it actually arrived, when our daughter, our youngest child, was about to leave for college, it felt as if it had happened in the blink of an eye.

I know that for a lot of people, the prospect of being empty-nesters is sad, maybe even a little scary. But Amy and I were incredibly excited about it. We loved our children intensely and wanted them near us always. There wasn't a shred of doubt about that, and they knew it. At the same time, we'd always reminded them that we came first. In today's society, it seems that the boomerang effect of adult children returning home is more common than not. While Amy and I welcomed that possibility, we were elated at the opportunity to return to where it all started, just the two of us, navigating this whole new chapter of life. Unapologetically, and with our kids cheering us on every step of the way, we started making plans for that chapter.

Given how we'd lived our married life for more than twenty years, perhaps it's not surprising that, as we started to plan for being on our own again, Amy and I were like a couple of kids whose parents had left them alone in the house for the weekend. We had the whole place to ourselves. We had the whole *world* to ourselves.

We'd gotten a small taste of this back in April 2012 when we went to Thailand together, without the kids. Because of her success as an author, Amy was in demand for book tours throughout the country and the world. The majority of her trips took her away from home for only a couple of days. Others were longer and more exotic, and gave me a chance to reap the benefits of being married to a creative force who was in demand in many different settings.

Such was the case when we got to take that trip to Thailand on our own. Between her commitments, we spent a few days off the mainland on the magical island of Koh Kood, celebrating our twenty-first wedding anniversary. Koh Kood is as romantic as it gets. Crystal-clear water. Fresh, delicious food. No kids, no emails, no cars, nothing but time, time to be together, to marvel at where we were as well as who and what we'd become individually and as a couple since that blind date on July 2, 1989. If this is possible for two people who were already in love, Amy and I fell in love all over again on the island of Koh Kood.

From there it was back to the mainland, where Amy was enveloped with love and admiration by the International School Bangkok while I roamed the urban streets with my camera. I was feeling lucky, grateful, and excited about the future.

Needless to say, as the time approached for Paris to head off to college, we were getting increasingly excited about being able to focus just on us for the first time in years. To the surprise of, oh, no one, we created an Amy-initiated list of empty-nest plans that we were constantly adding to. In no particular order . . .

Travel with Ann and Paul (Amy's parents) on a trip to South Africa.

Live in a foreign city.

Go to Burning Man.

Apply for the Harvard Loeb Fellowship (Amy).

Tour Asia with Mother (Amy).

Go to Marfa in Texas to see the "Marfa Lights."

Do writers' residencies in foreign schools (Amy).

Spend more time in New York.

Do more painting (Jason).

Do more social service.

We had a lot to do, and we couldn't wait to get started.

But first, Amy had committed to a trip to Washington, DC, for the National Book Festival at the Library of Congress. I was too slammed with work commitments to go with her to Washington, but she'd been allocated two tickets. So Amy did what Amy did; she reached out to her online community and initiated a contest, the winner of which would be her date to the event.

Her Facebook post read, "Would you like to be my 'plus one' at the Library of Congress National Book Festival gala dinner on Friday night, September 4th? I was told I could bring a guest and thought it would be fun to offer up the opportunity to a nice, book-loving human in the DC area. To put your name in the hat, simply chime in in the comment section by Wednesday 5PM CST . . ."

The winner, a lovely woman from Virginia, told me later that going to this event with Amy was "one of the most exciting days of my life." She also said that Amy had to excuse herself at one point because she was having stomach discomfort and needed to pick up some over-the-counter medication, something that I didn't learn until much later.

The next day, September 6, 2015, Amy called me before she boarded the plane for her scheduled flight home to Chicago. She was having pain in her right side, and she'd called her doctor, who suggested I take her to the emergency room when she got back.

It shook me up—twenty-six years together, and this was a first. I tried to ease Amy's mind, and mine, by theorizing that it was probably appendicitis.

I picked her up at the airport and drove her straight to the emergency room at Northwestern Memorial Hospital. After the obligatory hours of waiting, waiting, several diagnostic tests, and waiting, a baby-faced emergency room doctor sat us down to give us the results of the scan he'd ordered.

Yes, he said, the appendix was involved, but what was going on had nothing to do with appendicitis. Instead, Amy's appendix was mildly thickened with multiple nodules. Her lymph nodes, which he defined as a network of small structures throughout the body that filter fluids to help minimize toxins and neutralize infection, were enlarged. The liver was involved too.

It was obvious that this doctor hadn't had much experience at delivering upsetting news to patients. He was as nervous as we were, and to get it over with, he just kind of blurted out the word he'd been leading up to: "Tumor."

That word invaded Amy's body as well as our lives.

It seemed the scan was "suggestive" of a tumor, and she needed to get more testing right away.

What? *What?!*

We were completely silent for most of the drive home as the news set in. My mind was unsuccessfully scrambling to think of something wise, positive, and optimistic that I could say without my voice breaking. Amy was slowly letting her emotions catch up with the news that had just blindsided us.

It didn't really come crashing down on us until we got out of the car, grabbed Amy's luggage from her DC trip, and walked through our front door into the deafening stillness of our empty nest.

PART II

Loss

5

Something Is Not Right

We are secrets to each other
Each one's life a novel
No one else has read.
Even joined in the bonds of love
We're linked to one another
By such slender threads.

　　　　—Neil Peart*

Amy was freakishly gifted at wordplay, automatically and almost involuntarily seeing letters within words that formed other words. She saw an Exit sign and thought how nice it would be to have it read "Excite" instead. She thought "creation" was a stimulating, active, valuable time investment, as opposed to "reaction," which contains exactly the same letters and implies letting other people dictate how you're going to spend your life. The rest of us Rosenthals kept trying to pick up the skill, but even when it was staring us right in the face, we couldn't hold a candle to her.

But how much would we have given for her diagnosis to have been *acne*, tucked neatly into *cancer*, this abhorrent new word in our vocabulary?

---

* (I also quoted Mr. Peart in my high school yearbook. Simpler times.)

We immediately reached out to our considerable network to get the names of the best and the brightest oncology surgeons in the country. It turned out that two of them were right here in Chicago. We went to an appointment with the first of them on September 8, 2015, when the phrase "suspicious for metastasis" (aka "the cancer appears to be spreading") entered our vernacular.

Our second appointment was with the renowned Ernst Lengyel, MD, PhD, an expert in ovarian, cervical, and endometrial cancers, which was where our journey began in Ernst (I try, Amy). We went to see Dr. Lengyel on September 11, 2015, at the University of Chicago in Hyde Park, which soon become our new home away from home.

Surgery was scheduled just a few days later, on September 16, 2015. It was time to start notifying children and family, but that came with its own set of baffling questions—most notably, just how exactly were we supposed to give people this news out of nowhere? Of course, Amy and I hadn't been prepared either, but at least we'd been in the room(s) as the awful events unfolded and had had a chance to start processing them, together. Picking up the phone and calling with terrible news just felt so daunting.

Still, it's not until you're tested by life like this that you truly understand what it means to have a family that supports you no matter what. In addition to her exceptional parents, Amy's siblings were critical pieces of our lives. By this point, all three of her siblings had married people who were spectacular in their own right. Adding to the embarrassment of riches, there are twelve cousins (and some stepcousins) in the family, all of whom are connected to us and each other like (to stay with the medical theme) vertebrae. On my side, my sister Michel, who also lives in Chicago, is brilliant, creative, and loyal to me, Amy, and her nieces and nephews. My brother Tony—from my dad's second marriage but truly my brother—and his wife manage to stay very connected and generous to Amy, me, and our children from their home in New York. Our parents are different but incredibly alike, in that they each adored their offsprings' choices of mates so much that they considered Amy and me to be their very own kids.

We made it through those calls somehow, and of course received nothing but love and support and the reassurance that we were all in this together. Then we took a moment to brace ourselves for what was coming next.

There are a few challenges in life that seem unbearable, but is there one more daunting than having to tell our children that their mother has ovarian cancer? Even as I write that, I'm aware of how shortsighted it is. Men and women much braver than I risk their lives every day in defense of this country, and some of them never make it home. Jerry Sittser, author of the beautiful memoir *A Grace Disguised*, suffered a challenge when three generations of his family died instantly in a car crash. Even so, there was still no way around it—picking up the phone that day, and hiding my dread from Amy as best I could so she wouldn't have the added burden of comforting *me*, was the toughest test I ever thought I'd be faced with in my privileged lifetime.

We set up a conference call for all of us, kept our voices calm and confident, and filled them in on everything, from their mom's diagnosis to as many details as we knew about her upcoming surgery.

They were amazing—shocked, of course, and sad, and frightened, and completely thrown; but during our time with them on the phone, their end of the conversation pretty much boiled down to "You'll do great, Mom," and "How can we help?" and "Don't worry about us."

Amy was selfless in the call, focused (not for the last time) on how much she hated her illness causing any disruption in our children's young lives.

After we received the diagnosis, we became a cancer family forever. Amy went to work. It was never a battle, as some people describe it. She hated that analogy. This was not a game. It was not a war. Amy was a lover *and* a fighter, but in a methodical way. Of course, she made a list of all of the things we had to do over the next few days before surgery. Amy's overall attitude was one of taking care of business. She never displayed any self-pity for her predicament. "Why me?" was never part of her emotional state. Emotions were for later. Now it was all focus, drive, and determination.

For my part, it's interesting to look back on what was going on in my head at that time. I was just sad, not for myself (at least not yet) but for the depth of the pain that was being unavoidably inflicted on our kids. I wished there were a way for me to gather up all their pain and take it on myself. I would have done it in a heartbeat.

And yet as I moved beyond their pain, I found myself stuck between two different outlooks. On one hand, even though it still wasn't clear whether Amy's cancer was ovarian or fallopian, it was painfully clear how serious it was. It devastated, terrified, and overwhelmed me. It made me angry, and it made me feel impotent—my wife was in the worst trouble of her life, and I couldn't do a damned thing about it.

On the other hand, as I lay in bed wide awake the night before surgery, I remember being completely sanguine about the outcome. This wasn't just anyone who was being operated on the next day; this was Amy. Amy Krouse Rosenthal. No way would this woman who'd dedicated her life to goodness be stolen from us. This beautiful soul, the driving force behind an interactive short film project called *The Beckoning of Lovely*, had too much good to share and too much left to do to leave this earth unfinished. This bighearted, selfless lady, whose legacy color is yellow, the color of happiness, glory, and wisdom; this daughter who respected and admired her parents and in-laws; this revered sibling, this cherished wife, would not possibly be taken and leave such intense sorrow behind. No way. This woman, the perfect parent who adored her children, could not leave me to do it all alone.

My other half could not be taken. Without her, I'd be half the man I used to be.

6

Together We Are One

And as I sat there, I realized that the questions intersecting life, death, and meaning, questions that all people face at some point, usually arise in a medical context.

—*Paul Kalanithi*

God help the hospital that finds a member of the Krouse/Rosenthal family checking in as a patient.

Rudyard Kipling once observed, "For the strength of the pack is the Wolf, and the strength of the Wolf is the pack." And whatever our family was doing—from getting together on Sunday afternoons to swim, play games, talk, and eat to hibernating in Michigan, coloring, reading, and walking in the ravines, to supporting each other through a hospital experience—we gathered as a pack. We'd already ridden out ten births together, a couple of heart procedures, one bout of lung cancer, and several knee surgeries (four on my right knee alone!).

We probably overwhelmed a few hospital staffs, maybe even provided a little levity, in the way we didn't just assemble in waiting rooms but took them over.

On September 26, 2015, we overtook—or, to be more precise, hunkered down en masse in—a waiting room at the University of Chicago Hospital for a day none of our previous experiences had prepared us for: the endurance test that was Amy's surgery. They don't call them "waiting rooms" for nothing. We knew we had a long wait ahead of us, we just had no idea how long.

The day was a bit of a fog. For the most part, my confidence in the surgical team superseded those dark, occasional, inevitable "What if . . ." thoughts, and all of us in that room did an admirable job of buoying one another up with a steady stream of positive thoughts.

Amy was so strong; surely she could defy the odds. For years, after all, she had been a practicing yogi, dedicated to her ashtanga practice. She swam regularly at various times in her life. Her calves! She had strong legs that propelled her on walks, sometimes as long as two hours, carrying her from one part of the city to the other. Other than the potato chip addiction she inherited from her mother and a heavy hand with mayonnaise, she lived a healthy lifestyle.

Then, as the hours dragged on, there would be those long silences when we all withdrew into our own thoughts and overwrought nerves, and I'd pull out my notes and study the list of new medical terms that had suddenly invaded our vocabulary:

Total abdominal hysterectomy
Bilateral oophorectomy
Omentectomy
Lymph node dissection
Tumor debulking
Possible appendectomy
Potential damage to surrounding structures . . . bowel
Lymphedema

That's a lot of *ectomy*s for one operation. The etymology of the suffix *ectomy*, I'd learned, is from the Greek *ektomia*, "a cutting out of." Amy was little, five-one when she stood up very straight, and weighing in just north of one hundred pounds. How much could that tiny body handle? And why did it have to take so damned long?

Several millennia—i.e., nine hours—later there was a group exhale when Dr. Lengyel appeared, and a few of us were herded into a small consultation room.

He patiently, articulately explained everything.

All I heard was "Amy made it through surgery."

It still humbles me to look back on that man, that extraordinary doctor who'd had the focus and dedication to devote *nine hours* to increasing the chances of Amy living with a chronic disease, best-case scenario, rather than dying of cancer. Now, that's important work. That's worthwhile. That's essential. . . . While I was doing what with my life, exactly? Okay, I'd helped some people in my thirtysomething years as a lawyer, but had I come anywhere close to saving a life? No, I couldn't really say I had. But there are how many Dr. Ernst Lengyels? Not enough. He's a rare breed, and we were blessed that he was there for Amy when we so desperately needed him.

I don't think I really started breathing again until Amy opened her eyes in the recovery room. She was back. I never doubted it (except in those dark, awful "What if . . ." moments), but I couldn't believe it, either. I won't even pretend to know what it was like for her to wake up from having her insides removed and rearranged; I just knew that whatever it took for her to recover, and however long, I'd be right there with her. Because Amy was who she was, we both fed off the intensity of her determination to be her strong, healthy, vibrant self again.

We took our cues from her doctors when it came to her

physically healing at the right pace. It started with walking a few steps down the hallway and slowly progressed as the days went by to walking down the hall, touching the door at the end, and making the loop up the hall again until she was back in her bed. Baby steps, but every one of them seemed like a miracle.

Oh, there was one unexpected bump in the road—as a result of the lengthy surgery, Amy had suffered a femoral nerve injury. Translation: her leg was messed up, and she had limited use of it. While her doctors assured us that it wasn't an uncommon side effect of such intense surgical procedures and she'd very probably make a full recovery, it felt like just one more thing to be concerned about. We were optimistic at this point that Amy would beat ovarian cancer, but did this nerve injury mean she might end up being a cancer survivor with a permanent limp?

In the big picture, though, we agreed that we had much bigger fish to fry than worrying about the possibility of a limp. Dr. Lengyel's team included the brilliant and genteel Dr. John Moroney, who, even with the crazy busy schedule he maintained, took the time to meet our three children when they themselves wanted to talk about Amy's exact diagnosis. They had an honest conversation about her chances of survival and other questions on their minds. What a gift to have such a caring and talented man on our team.

Before long it was time for the next recommended course of treatment—chemotherapy. Ideally, chemotherapy in a warm climate. The duration of the protocol advised by the medical team: sixteen weeks. Sixteen weeks would plunge us into the heart of winter. In Chicago. Which no one in their right mind has ever described as a warm climate. If what Amy needed was going through chemo where it was warm, where she could build up her strength by being outdoors taking walks, maybe even swimming, that's exactly what Amy would get, if we had to move heaven and earth to make it happen.

Again, we're lucky people: Amy's folks, Ann and Paul, were Florida residents. Our oncologist gave us a referral there, and we researched to find her the best facility and health-care provider Florida had to offer.

The thought of not being right by Amy's side every minute of those sixteen weeks was almost unfathomable to me. But this wasn't about me, it was all about her, and whatever she needed. Ann and Paul were thrilled at the opportunity to care for her, and Amy was enormously relieved and grateful to have her parents' open, adoring arms waiting for her in the Sunshine State. As for me, I'd just have to make some adjustments, shift some priorities, and make it work. I'd commute to Florida every chance I got, which would turn out to be every weekend, and an occasional week here and there. Yes, my work would suffer. Yes, there would definitely be some financial stress. And yes, in the big picture, with the stakes being Amy's illness and ultimately her life, those concerns were beside the point.

We flew to Florida—Amy, me, and our loyal family dog Cougar by Amy's side.

Time out for a brief, important, long-overdue introduction:

The kids were roughly eleven, nine, and seven when Amy's assistant at the time, Emily, rescued a beautiful black Lab mix puppy from a homeless woman who was selling puppies out of a box at a gas station for $15 apiece. Justin had a dog-walking business at the time and discovered Cougar sitting in Emily's car outside our house. As it turned out, Emily couldn't keep him in her apartment, for some roommate- or landlord-related reason. So . . . she asked if we could care for the little guy until she was able to make other arrangements. I'm sure you can hear Justin now: "Mom, Dad, can we pleeeeeeeeeease?!" We agreed to keep the puppy for the night, but Amy and Justin were leaving town the next day. Amy trusted me to make the right decision while they were gone. You know the rest—we fell hopelessly in love with him, we named him Cougar, and from that first night on there were six "Rosies" instead of five.

Drawing of the 6 "Rosies."

I'd been struggling with insomnia for years, so it came as no surprise that sleep was even harder now. Only instead of the imagined problems I used to worry about, I had something far more substantial and real to focus on in Amy's illness. I'd kick myself for all the stupid things I used to worry about that were irrelevant, unimportant, and downright trivial compared to what was going on now. And it was impossible to think about what was happening to her without adding in uncertainty about whether what I was doing was what I *should* be doing with the limited time I had left in this life. I know that many men my age, even those who haven't been sucker punched with the devastating illness of a loved one, go through the existential struggle about what really matters in life. I'd been battling mine for years, but after this brief separation from Amy, I knew I needed to stop thinking about it and start taking some kind of positive step away from the emptiness of work and toward the things that really mattered in life.

Letting go began with ending my regular attendance at my office in downtown Chicago. It's a large space I shared with other lawyers who, like me, were solo practitioners or had small partnerships. This is a truly amazing group of professionals and human beings. From the moment the news of Amy's diagnosis spread through the office, every one of those people had my back. They offered to stand in for me at court appearances, my staff took over the day-to-day requirements of running a law practice, and they regularly checked in to ask how Amy and I were doing and what they could do to help. What wonderful people they are, stepping up like that for someone in need. I hope I've sufficiently thanked them for lending a hand during this difficult stretch and keeping me going when I wasn't one bit sure I had it in me.

Once I'd loosened up on my office hours and Amy had settled in to her new chemo routine in Florida, I became a professional commuter. I'd spend a few days a week in Chicago taking care of unavoidable business and checking in with our kids, family, and friends. Then I'd be off to Florida for the rest of the week. It was demanding and stressful on the body and the mind, but I wouldn't have had it any other way.

Those Florida visits involved a lot more than just throwing some clothes in a suitcase and hopping on a plane. If it was even possible, my already incalculable love and admiration for Amy were growing stronger with every minute of every day.

I never went to see her without bringing her an illustrated book. Art helped to fill her up, and she was incredibly connected to the illustrators she used for her own books.

Some of the books I brought to Amy in Florida.

I recently came across a note I wrote to her when I'd decided to be by her side regardless of life and work in Chicago:

> *You asked me recently if there is anything I want to tell you in light of the shitstorm that has hit us. I want to say I love you. Not in the way I say it every day, like "love you," as in "see you after work and remember while I am gone that I truly love you." But in the way that I never have loved nor will ever love anyone again in my life. In the way that you complete me fully. In the sense that you gave me support and confidence and intimacy in a way that those three words are the only way to explain it. In a way that allows me to be me and you to be you because of the love I have for you. Meaning, you are my soul and it would be nice if we can beat this battle and love each other for a long time—as our love should be.*
>
> *I will be with you for this round of treatment, because I love you.*

7

Is It All a Bunch of Crap?

I don't wanna live like this, but I don't wanna die.

—Ezra Koenig

Settling in with Amy, Ann, Paul, and Cougar in Florida felt exactly right. Work would suffer. So would finances. Too bad. As far as I was concerned, at this point I couldn't afford to be anywhere else.

Amy's chemotherapy was progressing on schedule, but we were open to exploring any other options we could add that might help to stave off the relentless cancer cells that were trying to infiltrate her body. And according to the internet, there were a lot of them. Have you ever googled what ginger, curcumin (the active ingredient in turmeric), and mushroom extract do for cancer patients? Try it. The amount of information is exhaustive, and, as we all know, if it's on the internet, it must be true.

Ginger: "Ginger is 10,000 times stronger than chemo in cancer research model"; "Ginger causes cancer cells to commit suicide" (interesting choice of words there!).

How about curcumin? "It has shown incredible promise in the prevention of cervical cancer, the leading cause of cancer death among women in developing nations"; "Experimental studies have identified curcumin's ability to prevent metastasis in breast cancer, lung cancer, liver cancer, thyroid cancer, ovarian cancer and prostate cancer."

Hey, what about 'shrooms? "There is good evidence that mushrooms are among the most powerful functional food in a growing cancer-fighting and cancer-preventing arsenal"; "Known for its immune-building and anti-aging virtues, more recent research highlights the antibody-mediating, multi-mechanistic power that makes the Reishi (mushroom) a super cancer-fighter."

Eastern, Western, holistic, homeopathic, woo-woo, you name it—we were on board for trying it, as long as it couldn't hurt. There was a health food store in the neighborhood, and they must have thought they had a couple of ginger, turmeric, and reishi mushroom junkies on their hands. Oh, and a specific type of almond butter, and the ingredients for the "packed with purpose" muffins Amy made in batches and ate for breakfast every morning, as our friend Ava recalls. But *zero* sugar of any kind, and absolutely no alcohol. (Damn, a few sips of vodka would have been nice at the end of these brutal days.)

And through it all, I kept it very much to myself that my faith in alternative remedies, and traditional ones, and even my faith in general, were becoming intensely strained as I watched Amy physically disappearing right in front of my eyes.

How dare . . . somebody . . . something . . . do this to her? How much harder did she have to try to earn back the health and the life she never took for granted for a single moment? She wasn't just going through chemotherapy and following every order from her doctors and every lead she was given on how to beat this. She was also working day and night, between chemo sessions, on her latest memoir, *Textbook Amy Krouse Rosenthal*.

All this, and it still wasn't enough? If there was a God, she must have been sleeping on the job this time.

There were some bright spots along the way in the stress of this new life we were living, but none of them was more memorable than Thanksgiving of 2015. Justin, Miles, and most of our family were gathering in Florida at Ann and Paul's to spend the holiday together. We wanted all of them with us, of course; there was just a practicality/logistics issue when it came to our daughter, Paris. She was in college in British Columbia, an almost six-hour flight away. Since Canada doesn't celebrate our Thanksgiving, Paris didn't have a long holiday break ahead of her, and Amy decided that twelve hours on a plane over a brief Thanksgiving weekend was far too arduous a trip for our daughter to go through.

I "agreed." Then I snuck off by myself, called Paris, and we made all the arrangements.

Trying to act nonchalant on the appointed day wasn't easy, let me tell you. But finally I got a text from Paris, letting me know she'd arrived, and she was waiting exactly where we'd agreed she'd be. Then I asked Amy to come with me to look at something in the garage.

Sporting her wig and her favorite knit hat, Amy stepped into the garage. The instant she saw her beautiful little girl standing there, she lost all control of her body and began screaming, "Oh, my God, oh, my God, oh, my God!" over and over again. The pure joy, love, and appreciation in their long, tight embrace is an exquisite emotional snapshot that will stay with me forever.

Like Thanksgiving, holidays and other special occasions became more and more precious as time went on. The most memorable during this time was my trip to Florida on the day of the Oscars in 2016.

I'd grown up watching the Oscars with my mom and sister, and Amy and I never missed them either. Many years running, I would be on the phone with my sister, "watching" together. These were loving phone calls where we often said nothing, just enjoyed the ceremony in mutual silence. It was more a tradition than a cause for a huge celebration. We didn't throw viewing parties or glue ourselves to the TV to see what the stars were wearing on the red carpet. We'd try to see all the nominated movies and enjoyed our annual tradition of pulling for them, or against them, to win the Academy Award.

Amy and I hadn't said a word about the Oscars that year, understandably; we had plenty of other, far more important things to talk about. But a couple of days before that particular trip, I noticed that if my flight landed on schedule, I'd arrive at the house just in time for the telecast. So I decided to greet Amy with an invitation to be my date for our own private Academy Awards viewing party, and I boarded that plane wearing a tuxedo. Apparently it's not as uncommon as I would have thought to see a guy in a tux on a Southwest Airlines flight. No one commented, no one asked about it, no one even did a double take. Oh, well. The only reaction that mattered was Amy's, and I couldn't wait to see the surprised smile on her face when I showed up at the door in formal wear to share Hollywood's biggest night with her.

I think my jaw literally dropped open when my Uber pulled up to the house. I hopped out in my tuxedo, grabbed my bag, and, as the Uber drove away, found myself staring at a completely unexpected variation on the Gift of the Magi story—the walkway to the front door was covered with a red carpet.

Amy and I had shared a special connection since the night we met. Sometimes it was almost uncanny. Amy (and her mom!) were blown away by my having worn my tuxedo. Her reaction was sweet and loving. She was so happy.

Of course, along with the profound gratitude that we were still together to celebrate moments like these, we both contended with the constant unspoken fear that each might be the "last . . ."

On Amy's birthday, April 29, 2016, I was so overwhelmed with gratitude that I had to let it spill out on paper in a letter to her:

When I was at Anshe Emet as a boy, we had a crew called "The 51ers." Dave and Jeff were in it. Now, you and I form our own gang. The New 51ers, you and me at 51. And boy am I honored to be in this union with you.

To say that 50 was a brutal year is quite the understatement. Who knew what Rabbi Kudan meant when he said "in sickness and in health"? When we were 26 and getting married, certainly we did not think ahead to what came our way in 2015/16. Maybe we thought about comforting each other when we got the flu or had knee surgery. Not this.

I know people—you included—give me credit for helping you through surgery, chemo and recovery. Honestly, I could not have acted any other way. I just did what I know how to do. You, on the other hand, accepted this challenge in typical Amy fashion, "textbook" even. Who goes through chemotherapy and works 16-hour days? Amy. Look back. You never complained, ever. Today, we officially close this chapter and move on.

Because you are who you are, there is so much to look forward to this year. Is it cliché to say "You deserve it"? Well, whatever you believe, having a book in the #1 position on the New York Times bestseller list is quite an accomplishment. I mean, really, Margaret Wise Brown, Eric Carle, Mo Willems and AKR. Good company indeed. What a way to start your 51st year!

August 9th.* That certainly is also something to make your 51st year pretty darn exciting. It already is making things so exciting for you. I share your utter enthusiasm and anticipation for this process and all that comes with it.

I am so, so happy to be celebrating this day with you. Any occasion to honor you, I accept. I look forward to sharing so much with you, Amy. You make my life so full, so interesting, so loving, so fun and so fulfilling.

I just love you so very much.

Love, Jason

---

* August 9 was declared by the mayor to be Amy Krouse Rosenthal Day in Chicago. Amy planned an entire day at Millennium Park to commemorate the release of her latest memoir, Textbook Amy Krouse Rosenthal.

8

One Last Bash

I could be yours so true
I would be, I should be, through and through.
—*Nick Drake*

As life would have it, we had more to celebrate in the summer of 2016 than we'd dared to imagine—we got the news after the conclusion of her chemo treatment that Amy was in remission.

Our relief and excitement levels were off the charts. It's funny, even with the intensity of everything we'd been through, and the severity of Amy's disease, we briefly shifted from stressed-out overload into elated optimism.

Amy fell in love that summer with a Justin Timberlake song called "Can't Stop the Feeling." Her taste was normally a bit more solemn: Nick Drake, Elliott Smith, and Badly Drawn Boy come to mind. We decided to throw a celebratory dance party with that song as its theme. It was a euphoric multigenerational gathering, our kids, our friends, and their kids, eating and drinking and dancing the night away in our backyard. Amy was spectacular—who else just north of fifty could pull off a lime-green *Soul Train*–worthy one-piece? We toasted her, our friends and family, and life in general.

Then we went in for Amy's follow-up appointment and scan.

The scan showed that the malignancy was back, in her liver and her lymph nodes.

Our world came crashing down again.

Amy's medical team strongly recommended immunotherapy, which apparently borders on being the new normal in the treatment of many cancers. She started the protocol right away. The doctors were encouraging, and we let some cautious optimism creep in again.

Paris was with Amy in Chicago, and Justin returned to California, where he'd just moved. Miles was about to start his senior year of college, and the plan was that I would drive him and his belongings to Atlanta, about an eleven-hour journey. On August 17, 2016, a few days before we were scheduled to leave, Amy was admitted to the hospital. She was experiencing shortness of breath, and her blood pressure was an alarming, life-threateningly low 86 over 68.

They were able to stabilize her fairly quickly, but Miles and I were already talking about alternative plans to get him to Atlanta. Amy wasn't having it. I was taking him back to school, period, drive carefully, buh-bye. She desperately wanted as much normalcy for the kids as possible through this awful chapter of their and our lives. It would give her a sense of peace knowing they were doing "what they were supposed to be doing," and in Miles's case, that meant starting his senior year on time, keeping up with his coursework, and graduating right on schedule.

So Miles and I set out on our road trip.

Our white Ford was packed to the gills with Miles's belongings as we set off for our marathon journey. It seemed like yesterday that he, Amy, and I had taken this exact same pilgrimage to see our middle child off to the beginning of his college career. Where did the time go? What had I worried about back then that I thought was a big deal? Had I appreciated every precious, simple moment, when we were all so happy and healthy, as much as I should have? Probably not, without something like our current circumstance to compare it to. And now, if Amy weren't surrounded by family and more than competent healthcare providers in the hospital, could I have even brought myself to pull out of our alley, let alone travel eleven hours away? Probably. But only because she was right, it wouldn't do either of us any good to have such an important time in our kids' lives turned upside down by something they couldn't do a thing about.

Miles and I were approaching Nashville, roughly the seven-hour mark, when we got the call from someone in the family. I don't remember who. I just remember what they said: Amy wasn't breathing well. She might not be able to breathe on her own. Her doctors were thinking of intubating her, and they might have to put her in a medically induced coma that she might or might not come out of.

Message received. Loud and clear.

Thankfully, I was vaguely familiar with the area and the stretch of interstate we were on, and I knew we were close to the Nashville airport exit. We were there in minutes, veered off at the exit, and floored it into the airport entrance.

For the first time in my life, I chose the valet parking lane at the airport and screeched to a stop in front of the attendant. Miles and I jumped out of the car—it was packed from floor to ceiling with Miles's belongings—and I handed over the keys.

I explained the situation as quickly as humanly possible. "My wife, this young man's mother, is in the hospital in Chicago. We need to get on the next plane immediately. We have no idea when we'll be back."

Miraculously, I could tell by his nod and the look on his face that he understood. I owe that man a lot more than the thank-you and the tip I gave him.

Once inside the terminal, we ran to the Southwest counter. I knew they had several flights to Chicago per day, and that it was a relatively quick trip. I breathlessly explained the situation to the woman behind the counter, and she immediately got us on a flight that was leaving in thirty minutes. People are good, damn it! With this unbelievable angel's help, we were escorted to the front of the security line, ran to the gate, and made it on board with moments to spare.

Miles and I were pretty quiet on the flight, withdrawn into our anxiety with no real reassurance to offer each other. Thankfully, we weren't in the air for long, maybe an hour and a half at most. We sprinted off the plane in Chicago, jumped in a ride-share, and flew up Fifty-Fifth Street East to the University of Chicago Hospital. Astonishingly, we were in Amy's room within two hours of getting that initial phone call.

We were both weak with relief when we dashed into that room and found that Amy was stable. Phew! In fact, as luck would have it, she was *not* in a medically induced coma and *not* intubated. She was, however, wearing a breathing mask, something between Darth Vader and your father's sleep apnea machine, that covered her nose and mouth. The rest of the room was the sterile, ugly, impersonal "usual"—IV machine next to the bed, with a tube connected to a line in her arm; no clock; the whiteboard with the on-shift nurse's name; the sofa/visitor's bed; machines beeping at various intervals.

The breathing mask was scary, but nothing compared to the images I'd been trying to brace myself for. Amy's eyes opened to see Miles and me standing beside her, and I saw them widen through the clear plastic of the mask. I knew those eyes. That wasn't "Thank God you're here" I was seeing, it was anger. She was pissed! What were we doing there, when we should have been in Atlanta, unpacking the car and getting Miles settled in for school? She thought she'd made herself clear—this nightmare was bad enough without her children's lives being thrown completely off track because of it!

It was impossible not to smile a little. Typical AKR. After all she'd been through, Amy was still in there, full force. And before long she calmed down and told us how much it meant to her to wake up and find us with her.

As it turned out, what had almost cost Amy her life was severe sepsis/septic shock on top of her pulmonary issues. It was a rare reaction to immunotherapy, suffered by only about 3 percent of patients.

Immunotherapy was no longer an option. We were running out of alternatives.

Either in spite of all that or because of it, Amy had her heart set on traveling to Florida at the end of December to ring in 2017 with our family, so that's exactly what we did.

It still kind of amazes me how cute and alive Amy looks in this picture. Sure, a little thin, but so Amy. It's hard to wrap my head around the fact that this was her last time with the family in Florida, our last New Year's Eve together, and the final days when she was allowed to eat.

She wasn't about to let anything stop her from conducting another of her interactive experiments on that trip. She called it "Message in a Bottle," and it was a promise she made in her memoir, *Textbook Amy Krouse Rosenthal*: if her readers would send her good wishes, for themselves or someone else, she would place them in bottles and toss them out to sea.

Her readers responded with more than eight hundred messages in a few short months, and she filled six bottles with them. Then, as a family, to help Amy fulfill a promise she would never have broken, we gathered on the beach and threw the bottles into the ocean. It was such an essential part of her fabric to honor a commitment. If she set out to do something, it got done. And if you told Amy you were going to do something, she held you to it.

I clearly remember sitting on the beach with Amy once all the messages had been "delivered." She was exhausted, from walking along the shore in the sand, I'm sure, but even the simple act of tossing a bottle into the ocean would have depleted her. As we sat there silently together, I got it, and felt it with everything in me, that our time was limited. But I couldn't let myself give in to the grief of knowing that. My only purpose at that moment was to make my love, my wife, the mother of my children, the most extraordinary person I'd ever known, feel comfortable and comforted.

Ann, my mother-in-law, told me later that she could see the pain in my face in this picture. Looking at it now, I just feel a deep sense of love and profound connectedness.

We went through all the motions of a traditional New Year's Eve celebration, with champagne and even the countdown to midnight and the official start of 2017.

And then it was back to Chicago for Amy's next appointment with her oncologist.

It was a tense flight back to Chicago, anticipating that looming doctor's appointment. What was next for us? Were there any options left? Our oncologist had developed a close connection with Amy, and we knew that if there was anything left to be done, he would do everything in his power to make it happen.

The look on his face when he walked into the room said it all—the news wasn't good. Amy's CA125 levels, or tumor markers, were off the charts. She had a complete bowel obstruction that would prevent her from being able to eat solid foods.

It pained him to say it, but there was only one question left: Did we want to do hospice in the hospital, or at home?

Hospice. The last phase of a terminal illness. The focus is comfort and quality of life. The word *cure* is off the table.

Between inpatient and outpatient visits, we couldn't begin to count how many trips to the hospital we'd taken in the past twenty-four months. Inpatient stays were soul-crushing. In addition to the endless beeping and other alien sound effects, there was always a steady stream of well-meaning nurses bursting into the room, treating Amy like a child, calling her "Miss Amy" in a singsong way that went right up her spine.

It wasn't even a close call. If hospice was where we'd found ourselves, we'd do hospice at home. Our home. Full of love. Full of memories. With our family. With Cougar. With friends. Where Amy would die.

The message we got that day was not a complete shock. Our optimism, over the past couple of years at this point, was solid. Setbacks, as my good friend Mike Kates, a motivational personal trainer, was fond of saying, were setups for a comeback. We lived by that message in our own way. At the same time, we knew that Amy's diagnosis was likely terminal.

We got good at communicating on a much deeper level. Communicating in this way over the course of Amy's illness helped us deal with the certainty we were now facing: the end. We continued this intimacy after we were faced with this hospice decision. Our friend John Green reminded me of a Robert Frost quote, "The only way out is through," and Amy and I both had very specific jobs to finish. For Amy, she used the focus of her work to diminish the physical symptoms as well as the extreme emotional roller coaster that being faced with the end of life brought her. My job was clear. I had only one mission—to make Amy comfortable, to be her caretaker, to make her feel loved, and to make the last moments she had on this planet as tolerable as possible.

Amy and I had deep and emotional conversations about the end of life, parenting our children, and carrying on this life without her. We cried together. We did our best to make sure each of us was going to be okay. My mind was as active as the trading floor at the Chicago Mercantile Exchange before computers took over. The synapses in my brain signaled between considerations like hospice supplies and wound care and more existential issues such as what my life would be like as a fifty-two-year-old widower.

I set up my home office at the dining room table. Computer, files spread everywhere, it didn't matter, as long as I had a view of Amy. She and her laptop took up residence on the family room sofa, where she spent hours at a time wrapping up some final projects and working on something new that she was determined to finish, which would become her last published work.

I would be remiss not to mention that the stress of home hospice care was assuaged by the incomprehensible, undeniable commitment of each one of our children. The emotional and physical support I felt from them—and feel to this day—got me through the roughest of moments of home hospice. Paris took time off from school and was by her mom's side for the duration of our hospice experience. She was tender with her mommy every moment they were together.

Paris had become this incredible blend of stunningly beautiful and confidently strong. She'd somehow acquired a pair of magical blue eyes that pierce one's soul. Amy saw right into the center of those baby blues like no other person in our daughter's life. They shared inside jokes, phrases only the two of them understood, and unique skills like board games and list-making; they dreamed about each other and, when in each other's company, could often be found in an embrace.

From a very early age, Paris was tenacious. I remember instructing her when she was all of four years old, starting youth soccer: "Now, you know how you have lots of really good friends? Well, this ball right here is not your friend, so go get it!" or something to that effect. From that age forward, Paris was an above-average athlete. More important, it was the manner and method to her approach to sports that set her apart. As with other facets of her life, she was intensely hardworking and organized in her athletics. She stayed thirsty for methods of practicing and exercising that would make her better. As a high schooler, she loved to play basketball. We spent many days together alone in a Chicago Park District gym shooting and dribbling. She was hard on herself, but persistent. If she was going to play hoops, she was going to be the best version of herself at that sport. This characteristic of hers later applied to almost anything she set out to do. A culmination of her intense work ethic happened in her senior year of high school.

It was in her final year that the women's basketball team had to disband due to lack of interest by enough female athletes. So what did Paris do? She lobbied the administration and challenged the league rules to allow her to play the season on the boys' team. Correct. She became the first female player in the history of her school to play a basketball season on the boys' basketball team. At the end-of-the-year banquet, the parents gave her a standing ovation in recognition of her integrity, her hard work, and her sportsmanship throughout the season. This was typical of how she continues to conduct her life as a young adult today. Having Paris by my side during home hospice, as a tender supporter of her sick mother, as well as my health-care partner, helped me get through these very dark times.

And, as if to mimic the Marvel superheroes they have loved their entire lives, Justin and Miles would commute from out of state *every weekend*. Somehow, Miles, who was in his senior year of college, managed to graduate on time.

And then there was Justin. Take a cue from my eldest, Justin. He just knew how to communicate. From the moment he knew his mom was in hospice, he made a choice. He was not physically with us every day in hospice, but he connected with Amy every single day. That's right. He picked up the phone and called his sick mom each day to connect with her. When Amy talked with him, even if it was a brief moment, Amy lit up brighter than the most beautiful candle we had burning at the time. Such empathy from a young man—yes, a millennial—can teach us a thing or two about devotion, love, and connection.

If I had to make the same hospice decision all over again, there's no doubt about it, I'd still choose home. But parts of it bordered on unbearable. It was nothing compared to what Amy was going through, just as tough and emotionally challenging as life can get.

Basic daily activities. Who gives them a single thought? Pulling open the refrigerator door? Big deal. Going to bed? Walk into your bedroom, turn out the lights, and call it a day. Going to the bathroom? So what? Now, in our "new normal," those things all became hills to climb. Asking Amy to open anything, from the refrigerator door to a bottle of medicine, was like asking her to bench-press three hundred pounds. Walking upstairs to our bedroom was as exhausting for her as running a marathon. And during all those years we raised children together, not once in my wildest imagination did it occur to me that someday I'd need to use my diaper-changing skills on my wife. Did it ever enter my mind to complain or feel put-upon about any of it? Not even once. As much as it was to deal with, I just kept wishing I could do more.

Her inability to eat, which went on longer than anyone thought she'd be medically able to sustain, meant watching her shrink, right before my eyes. You know how your memory often consists of thousands of mental snapshots of different phases of your life? Well, during our home hospice experience, I only saw Amy as Amy, the love of my life, the woman I'd promised to take care of, in sickness and in health. As I look back, though, I can see how her steady weight loss and the disease that was eating her alive morphed her into "that look." You know it when you see it, that sunken, almost skeletal shadow you keep wishing you were just imagining; and somehow it only deepens your love from one day to the next.

If my memory serves me correctly, our doctors were vague about the subject of physical intimacy. I won't be. The possibility of being intimate in any physical way disappeared early on after Amy's diagnosis of a terminal illness. At the same time, I can honestly say that as Amy progressed through her disease, our intimacy actually became more profound than it had ever been at any point in our relationship. I still remember a moment during one of Amy's early hospital visits. I was in her hospital bed with her, holding her, with her tears falling on me, and she looked up at me and quietly said, "I just want to be normal again." That may sound like a simple, obvious plea. But coming from a superstrong woman like Amy, who never, *ever* complained or asked for anything, it was like a pure, honest, intense vision into her soul, and a whole new level of intimacy between us.

There was only one aspect of her home hospice care that, I admit it, I just couldn't deal with. Amy's bowel obstruction had caused a fistula—in the most basic layman's terms, an opening in the body where there shouldn't be one. Occasionally waste would make its way through that opening. It was extremely messy, very smelly, and almost unbearable to clean up after. Amy's mom and I did our best, but the wound care was way beyond my sensory limits and health-care skills.

In case you've ever wondered, there really are angels in this world. Ours was named Margaret. She was a wound-care nurse who'd worked for our dear friends Wendy and Jimmy. She took care of the wound, and the mess, and the smell without batting an eye. She couldn't have been more diligent, more professional, and more tender when it came to keeping Amy clean, which wasn't easy.

After Amy died, Margaret shared a story with me:

You may not remember this, but I'd just finished helping Amy in the shower. When she was all clean, we got out. I was in my clothes, of course, and I was as wet as she was. Amy had a big fluffy towel, and you offered me one, but I didn't really need it. Then, as we were walking back to your bedroom, she stopped at the closet and offered me one of her sweaters. Of course, Amy was a very small lady—tiny, in fact. And I'm not. I would have had to knit at least three of her sweaters together to fit me. But there she was, so sick, in so much pain, facing death, and she was worried about me getting cold. I've known a lot of good, kind people in my life, but I've never known one as kind as Amy.

This sentiment was one I would soon hear from countless people who reflected on Amy and the impact she made everywhere she went.

Of course, not everyone responds like the Margarets of the world. In fact, the variety of ways people react to a personal crisis like ours makes for a remarkable study of human nature. There's no doubt about it, it's a time when no one really knows what to do. Some instinctively get it. Others, out of either awkwardness or a complete lack of empathy, don't get it at all.

Family, of course, is everything; and this was their impending loss too. They were remarkable every step of the way. From my four-year-old nieces to my father-in-law, Amy and I could not have felt more support. To a person, they all knew what to say, how to behave, when to gather around us, and when to give us space.

You know how in life you have those few true friends, that handful of special people you can tell anything to, they can do the same with you, and no matter what, you'll always be there for each other? If you're lucky, you have one or two. Amy and I were *really* lucky—we had several.

Then there are those good friends you see and/or talk to regularly. You enjoy each other's company. You have long, chatty phone conversations, you make social plans, and you reminisce about the shared experiences that brought you together in the first place.

There are also those friends you'll always feel fond of and connected to, even if, for no other reason than the busyness of life, years go by when you're out of touch.

And with very rare exceptions they all, in every category, found a way to step up, just be there, and teach me valuable, lifelong lessons about the inherent goodness of the human race.

One of those exceptions happened on one of the rare occasions when I went to my downtown office to check in. As I was crossing the street, I saw an acquaintance coming straight at me. I'd known him for years. His wife had known Amy since childhood. Our kids went to grade school and summer camp together. It was immediately clear from the look on his face that he desperately wanted to say something to me, but as we got close enough to engage in a bro hug or a handshake, the most amazing thing happened: nothing. Not a word. Not a gesture. Instead, we stopped for a brief moment, he gave me a blank stare, and we were both on our way again in a flash. A word of advice if you have a friend whose loved one is dying: SAY SOMETHING. ANYTHING. It doesn't have to be that hard. "Man, I am so sorry" is good. "I am thinking about you" works. But total silence and darting away as fast as you can is what I'll politely call poor form, and your friend (in this case, me) won't forget it.

I'd also strongly dissuade you from saying things like "Give me a call" or "Let's get together," especially without following up. That puts the responsibility for the first move on the person who's already grieving and on total overload, and no matter how well-intentioned, it ends up feeling like one more burden. It's a much better idea to call with an already-set plan. "Dinner. My place. 7:00 p.m. Saturday." Maybe an added, "I'll pick you up." Even if the response is "No, thanks," you can count on it that the gesture mattered and was appreciated.

What is a legitimate offer to help a person who's grieving? Certainly that is difficult to say, and depends upon your relationship to the person who has experienced a loss. For example, many people wanted to reach out to me and meant well in doing so. However, "Hey, man, let's get a beer some time" is not, in my mind, a real offer. It puts the onus on the person who is going through way too much to be the one to make plans. My mind was clogged with impossible thoughts of sadness, loss, loneliness, and a variety of other emotions. I was in no place to make social plans. Something along the lines of "Jason, I know you are going through so much, let's meet for a beer at Union Pizzeria on Chicago Ave Thursday at 6:00 after work. I'll be at the bar with a beer. If you are up for it, great, you can count on my being there" sounds solid. Clear. A specific time and place. Listen, the worst thing that can happen is that I don't show up. Try again. Maybe "Hey, bro, I will be at your place with a six-pack of Gumballhead Monday night. If you don't feel like hanging out, I totally understand—still, take the brews. I hope you will feel up for a quick visit." Again, the worst-case scenario is that I don't even answer the door! No biggie. Leave the beverages. And keep trying.

Oh, and also, that tilt of the head with a furrowed brow, or a slight frown with a little headshake—uh-uh. Please don't do that. I know you're sad. I know you feel badly for me and Amy and our family. But pity is the last thing we need.

One close friend of mine texted Grateful Dead lyrics to me every week, all of them on the theme of the eternal nature of deep love. "You know my love will not fade away" was a regular. Such a simple, powerful way to connect with a friend who just needs the feel of a familiar hand on their shoulder.

A high school friend wrote me a note in which he confessed that he had no idea what to say, and yet said it beautifully: "Know that I don't write this kind of letter often. But I have learned not to doubt myself (or buy schmaltzy Hallmark sympathy cards). I think people worry about what to say to someone when they have lost someone dear in their life. . . . Amy seems like she would have said just write what you want to and be real. That's what I hope I've done here." Amen, brother, you definitely did. I could go on, but I think you get it.

One of our friends, Brian, showed up every Saturday morning while Amy was in hospice, always just to drop off three yellow items. Amy's connection to the color yellow was especially illustrated in *The Beckoning of Lovely*, a project of community and connectedness you can find on YouTube, where Amy entered Millennium Park carrying a yellow umbrella, which became her legacy symbol. Brian's weekly yellow gifts ranged from blow-up plastic duckies to balloons to mustard to anything else he could find on a thoughtful search through the dollar store. He never expected any kind of reciprocation. He never asked to see Amy, or expected to, but I was always the beneficiary of a bear hug if I was available when he stopped by.

One of my sweet nieces sent me simple postcards every once in a while, just to stay connected through our mutual heartbreak and let me know she was thinking about me.

And here's a really easy, affordable way to offer comfort and support to a friend who's in the process of losing a loved one, and maybe even give them a little smile. I recently attended a conference where a woman named Emily McDowell spoke about her company, which, among other things, really fills a void in the greeting card industry. They create cards for those moments when you don't have the first clue what to say but don't want to thoroughly nauseate yourself and the person receiving it. "There is no good card for this. I am so sorry" and "Please let me be the first to punch the next person who tells you everything happens for a reason" are two of my favorites.

Now that's more like it.

Whatever tough moments and reactions we encountered along the way, there was no doubt that in-home hospice was the right decision for us, particularly because of how we were able to create a warm and comfortable space for Amy. No one has ever used the simile "as beautiful as a hospital room," which is why we chose to make the home hospice experience as beautiful as it could possibly be. If you ever find yourself in the same position, take it from me, it makes a difference. Knowing the story is ending soon makes every word on those final pages that much more important, after all.

We organized people into groups of visitors, to keep Amy from being overwhelmed at any given time. We had a "Krouse Night" with her parents and three siblings. They sang their family song, and weak as she was, Amy joined in. On a separate night, loving, loyal, lifelong friends of Amy's came and regaled us with stories about her and us, from her high school years to her nervous anticipation about my calling her after our first date.

Amy and I had always shared an almost rabid love of music, and we had a variety of musicians come to our house and play for her. World-renowned blues guitarist and friend Dave Specter performed a stunning rendition of George Harrison's "While My Guitar Gently Weeps." Classical musicians serenaded her with stringed-instrument arrangements. A pianist with an angelic voice came every week, having learned the words and music of favorite songs I'd requested. Every one of these performances was weighted with meaning—not just for us but unexpectedly for the performers as well. Every one of those generous, gifted people told me later that performing for us was one of the most meaningful gigs they'd ever played.

For some reason, I became insistent that our home and lives be infused with candles. Their glow is ethereal, obviously, filling a room with an alive, flickering light that's always changing. Candles of various sizes also seemed to me to represent the uniqueness of the human form. The different shapes, sizes, fragrances, wicks burning with their own unique intensities, the inevitability of their burning out, all became icons of humanity and its frailty. Yes, I was witnessing this frailty every minute of every day, right before my eyes, but the candles gave it a certain grace and elegance that spoke to me. Being at home for long stretches of time, I started making candles of my own. Soon our family room and living room became a Rosenthal chandlery. Any container would do—an old soup can stripped of its label, a mason jar, an old jelly jar, existing candleholders that had burned all the way down—you name it, it was a candidate for the next homemade candle. It became a creative outlet in an otherwise dark time, something I could do when it felt as if there were so many things I couldn't, no matter how desperately I wanted to.

Then along came Valentine's Day. To celebrate us, and all that "us" meant, on this Hallmark-manufactured day, I peppered the house with love notes. I took blank sheets of music paper, filled pages of it with the lyrics to some well-known as well as favorite love songs, and posted them all over the house. I know her perception of what was going on around her was getting dim, but I'm still certain Amy saw them all and felt them in that infinite part of her that understood everything.

9

I'm That Guy

There were signs and signals,
even if they couldn't read them yet.
Perhaps three years ago
or just last Tuesday
a certain leaf fluttered
from one shoulder to another?
Something was dropped and then picked up.
Who knows, maybe the ball that vanished
into childhood's thicket?

  —*Wisława Szymborska*

Of course, I knew Amy had been spending a lot of time writing on her laptop, and I knew that whatever it was, she was fiercely determined to finish it. But in my wildest dreams, I never imagined this, published in the March 3, 2017, issue of the *New York Times*:

You May Want to Marry My Husband

by Amy Krouse Rosenthal

I have been trying to write this for a while, but the morphine and lack of juicy cheeseburgers (what has it been now, five weeks without real food?) have drained my energy and interfered with whatever prose prowess remains. Additionally, the intermittent micronaps that keep whisking me away midsentence are clearly

Illustration by Brian Rea.

not propelling my work forward as quickly as I would like. But they are, admittedly, a bit of trippy fun.

Still, I have to stick with it, because I'm facing a deadline, in this case, a pressing one. I need to say this (and say it right) while I have a) your attention, and b) a pulse.

I have been married to the most extraordinary man for 26 years. I was planning on at least another 26 together.

Want to hear a sick joke? A husband and wife walk into the emergency room in the late evening on Sept. 5, 2015. A few hours and tests later, the doctor clarifies that the unusual pain the wife is feeling on her right side isn't the no-biggie appendicitis they suspected but rather ovarian cancer.

As the couple head home in the early morning of Sept. 6, somehow through the foggy shock of it all, they make the connection that today, the day they learned what had been festering, is also the day they would have officially kicked off their empty-nesting. The youngest of their three children had just left for college.

So many plans instantly went poof.

No trip with my husband and parents to South Africa. No

reason, now, to apply for the Harvard Loeb Fellowship. No dream tour of Asia with my mother. No writers' residencies at those wonderful schools in India, Vancouver, Jakarta.

No wonder the word cancer and cancel look so similar.

This is when we entered what I came to think of as Plan "Be," existing only in the present. As for the future, allow me to introduce you to the gentleman of this article, Jason Brian Rosenthal.

He is an easy man to fall in love with. I did it in one day.

Let me explain: My father's best friend since summer camp, "Uncle" John, had known Jason and me separately our whole lives, but Jason and I had never met. I went to college out east and took my first job in California. When I moved back home to Chicago, John—who thought Jason and I were perfect for each other—set us up on a blind date.

It was 1989. We were only 24. I had precisely zero expectations about this going anywhere. But when he knocked on the door of my little frame house, I thought, "Uh-oh, there is something highly likable about this person."

By the end of dinner, I knew I wanted to marry him.

Jason? He knew a year later.

I have never been on Tinder, Bumble or eHarmony, but I'm going to create a general profile for Jason right here, based on my experience of coexisting in the same house with him for, like, 9,490 days.

First, the basics: He is 5-foot-10, 160 pounds, with salt-and-pepper hair and hazel eyes.

The following list of attributes is in no particular order because everything feels important to me in some way.

He is a sharp dresser. Our young adult sons, Justin and Miles, often borrow his clothes. Those who know him—or just happen to glance down at the gap between his dress slacks and dress shoes—know that he has a flair for fabulous socks. He is fit and enjoys keeping in shape.

If our home could speak, it would add that Jason is uncannily handy. On the subject of food—man, can he cook. After a long day, there is no sweeter joy than seeing him walk in the door, plop a grocery bag down on the counter, and woo me with olives and some yummy cheese he has procured before he gets to work on the evening's meal.

Jason loves listening to live music; it's our favorite thing to do together. I should also add that our 19-year-old daughter, Paris, would rather go to a concert with him than anyone else.

When I was working on my first memoir, I kept circling sections my editor wanted me to expand upon. She would say, "I'd like to see more of this character."

Of course, I would agree—he was indeed a captivating character. But it was funny because she could have just said: "Jason. Let's add more about Jason."

He is an absolutely wonderful father. Ask anyone. See that guy on the corner? Go ahead and ask him; he'll tell you. Jason is compassionate—and he can flip a pancake.

Jason paints. I love his artwork. I would call him an artist except for the law degree that keeps him at his downtown office most days from 9 to 5. Or at least it did before I got sick.

If you're looking for a dreamy, let's-go-for-it travel companion, Jason is your man. He also has an affinity for tiny things: taster spoons, little jars, a mini-sculpture of a couple sitting on a bench, which he presented to me as a reminder of how our family began.

Here is the kind of man Jason is: He showed up at our first pregnancy ultrasound with flowers. This is a man who, because he is always up early, surprises me every Sunday morning by making some kind of oddball smiley face out of items near the coffeepot: a spoon, a mug, a banana.

This is a man who emerges from the mini mart or gas station and says, "Give me your palm." And voilà, a colorful gumball appears. (He knows I love all the flavors but white.)

My guess is you know enough about him now. So let's swipe right.

Wait. Did I mention that he is incredibly handsome? I'm going to miss looking at that face of his.

If he sounds like a prince and our relationship seems like a fairy tale, it's not too far off, except for all of the regular stuff that comes from two and a half decades of playing house together. And the part about me getting cancer. Blech.

In my most recent memoir (written entirely before my diagnosis), I invited readers to send in suggestions for matching tattoos, the idea being that author and reader would be bonded by ink.

I was totally serious about this and encouraged submitters to be serious as well. Hundreds poured in. A few weeks after publication in August, I heard from a 62-year-old librarian in Milwaukee named Paulette.

She suggested the word "more." This was based on an essay in the book where I mention that "more" was my first spoken word (true). And now it may very well be my last (time shall tell).

In September, Paulette drove down to meet me at a Chicago tattoo parlor. She got hers (her very first) on her left wrist. I got mine on the underside of my left forearm, in my daughter's handwriting. This was my second tattoo; the first is a small, lowercase "j" that has been on my ankle for 25 years. You can probably guess what it stands for. Jason has one too, but with more letters: "AKR."

I want more time with Jason. I want more time with my children. I want more time sipping martinis at the Green Mill Jazz Club on Thursday nights. But that is not going to happen. I probably have only a few days left being a person on this planet. So why am I doing this?

I am wrapping this up on Valentine's Day, and the most genuine, non-vase-oriented gift I can hope for is that the right person reads this, finds Jason, and another love story begins.

I'll leave this intentional empty space below as a way of giving you two the fresh start you deserve.

With all my love, Amy

When I first read Amy's brilliant piece, I was blown away by the prose. I felt humbled that the last project she worked on, literally from her deathbed, was about me and for me. "Well, this is brilliant," I thought initially. "If it gets published, great. If not, at least Amy had the time to get it done." It's part of the life of a writer that it's impossible to predict how far a completed piece will go, if anywhere. Zero part of me imagined what would happen once her Modern Love column was published in the *New York Times*.

I recognized the traits from our very private life that Amy wrote about in her essay. We did not need to shout to the heavens how we felt about each other during the course of our long marriage together. We knew it. However, when she got her diagnosis, we began to speak about life after Amy. In those conversations, she encouraged me to carry on, to find someone else, that she wanted happiness and a long life for me with someone new. I was unable to process that reality until much later, so my reaction to her words at that point was always along the lines of "Okay, Amy, thank you. I understand how you feel." And in typical AKR fashion, she'd say something like "But please wait a few months . . . ," always infusing the challenges of life with humor.

Reading Amy's words again is as overwhelming as people's reaction to the piece when it first came out. It conjures up the emotions from that time, because behind so many of the qualities she comments on, I don't just see me, I see us. Those memories of cheese and olives, of the mini-sculpture that still sits on my shelf, of the Sunday morning smiley faces . . . those are memories of *us*. Sure, I did those things, but I did them for Amy. It didn't strike me until much later that embedded in those memories are seeds that go all the way back to our marriage goals and ideas list. They are parts of me that didn't emerge fully formed but instead grew out of my love for her and our love for each other.

More than anything, though, the shared DNA here is that drive for "more" that Amy speaks of. In so many ways, that was the essence of our time together, a hunger to be together in whatever way possible.

And yet even at the end of her life, there were surprises.

One evening when we were deep in the throes of hospice, I stepped out of the house—a rare event at this point—to make a trip to the grocery store. The store was close to home, so I took the opportunity to get some fresh air and walked there. Our house is located on a tree-lined street on the north side of Chicago, with a brick-paved front area and a black wrought iron picket fence, kind of a modern Tom Sawyer deal.

I was gone for maybe thirty minutes. I walked home in a quiet dusk. Streetlights had just come on. The peace and the beauty gave me a welcome exhale.

Then, as I approached the house, I came to a complete stop and just gaped. I even wondered if I was experiencing some sleep-deprived, stress-induced hallucination. Somehow, in the half hour I'd been gone, someone had tied a row of yellow umbrellas to the thirty-eight or so feet of our fence. They were evenly spaced, open, glistening in the fading dusk. I'd never seen anything like it, not even in a movie or a museum.

I raced into the house, and Paris and I assisted Amy to the front door to see this incredible vision. Depleted and frail as she

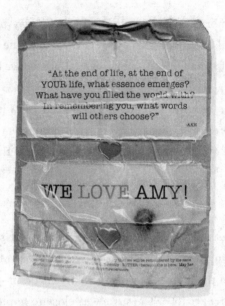

"At the end of life, at the end of
YOUR life, what essence emerges?
What have you filled the world with?
In remembering you, what words
will others choose?"

-AKR

WE LOVE AMY!

This sign marked the scene I returned to.

was, she was still able to marvel at it. She didn't say a word, she just stood there, with help, her eyes wide, and she smiled.

Possibly the most amazing thing of all—it was done in completely anonymity. No one ever took credit for it. To this day, I have no idea who gave us the gift of that unforgettable work of art.

Whoever you are, "Thank you" doesn't begin to express it.

And thank you, human race, for the goodness that goes unacknowledged far too often.

Looking back, it's become especially clear to me that much of the generosity that was showered on Amy during this impossibly difficult time was the result of the immeasurable generosity she showered on the rest of us. Somehow, with that frail, dying body, she found the strength to pay attention to everyone close to her—her family and close friends—and give them each a special moment to remember her by and tie her to them forever. A last conversation. A final thought. An assurance that everything would be okay, that she knew death was coming, and that she wasn't afraid. We all recall how at peace she was with the fact that she'd done everything medically possible and was ready for her transition, and she still found the strength to take care of us, while *she* was in hospice.

What a gift to have had these moments, and why shouldn't the rest of us have them now, while we're still healthy? What are we waiting for? How arrogant of us to believe there will always be "more time."

Seizing on the depth of this message was our eldest son, Justin. His new job brought him to California and a foray into the entertainment business. Despite his brutal schedule and the impeccable work ethic that had become a solid part of his values as a young adult, he traveled home to be with Amy every Friday on the red-eye flight. Incredibly, he was back at work on Monday. Justin intuitively knew how precious time was at this point in Amy's life. He battled the physical exhaustion to make certain to spend time with his mom. Time that was clearly running out.

Even though Amy's days of eating solid foods were over, she had her brother bring his daughter over and threw her a Dorito party to celebrate her second birthday. As a lifelong chipaholic, Amy's reputation preceded her when it came to her passion for the savory snacks. The joy on little Sadie's face was palpable as the three of them enjoyed their chip party.

She put on a corkscrew show for our nephew. In case you've never tried it, here's how Amy did it, after noticing that corkscrews bear a vaguely acceptable resemblance to human beings: she shone a light behind our corkscrew to create a shadow on the wall and then had the animated corkscrew shadow puppet tell her nephew a story about how much she loved each and every one of her siblings' children, even though there were so many of them.

She cooked a favorite meal for her sister's children.

She sat with her siblings, detailing to each of them why she admired them as people and parents, and asked them to please step in for our kids if they observed a "parenting moment" that I might happen to miss.

She discussed each one of our children with her family and close friends to make sure they'd have all the help and support they needed when they lost their mother—as if there was any question that our kids would ever be at a loss for unconditional love with such a close-knit group around them.

She reminded them to be there for me. We all understood how important it was at that point to say all those things that "go without saying."

In other words, she did absolutely everything in her power to leave no unfinished business, let us know she was confidently, fearlessly, peacefully ready to leave, and see to it that we were as ready as we could be too.

Then again, no matter how realistically prepared you think you are, no matter how many times you've played out that inevitable moment in your mind to brace yourself, it turns out that there's no such thing as "ready."

10

The End

Why did God create people if he knew they were going to die someday?

—*Justin Krouse Rosenthal, age ten*

There are images of those final days that continue to haunt me.

Walking backward to our bathroom, holding Amy up as she put one tentative foot in front of the other, her little legs barely able to hold her up. Praying every baby step of the way that I was holding her tightly enough that she wouldn't fall over, but not so tightly that I could hurt her. I'm not such a big guy, but my arms looked and felt so healthy compared to her frail body.

Confusion, delirium, and uncharacteristic restlessness. Out-of-character requests. I'd been warned that all those things might happen. Expecting them didn't make them any less scary. Amy's fistula had prevented her from indulging in her very favorite daily activity—taking a long, hot bath. One day when it was just the two of us, she insisted, out of nowhere, on getting in the tub. I wasn't about to say no to her about anything at that point, so I ran just a bit of water and gently lifted her into the tub. Another time, something called "terminal agitation" kicked in—a frightening involuntary movement of the limbs that may occur near the end of life. Again, not unusual for doctors and hospice workers, maybe, but terrifying for those of us who've never seen it before. I can still see it in my mind, sometimes without even closing my eyes. It's a hard one to shake off.

So many questions I did not know the answers to overwhelmed me at the end of our time in home hospice. Was there anything I could do to relieve these awful symptoms? What was she thinking as she straddled the fence between life and death? Was she aware of what her body was going through? Would this blue medicine, aka morphine, help quiet her and ease her pain, or could a dropper of this clear liquid help her rest?

I wanted it to end for her, and I never wanted to let her go.

And then there's the sequence of events that lingers most painfully.

On March 13, 2017, Amy and I were lying in bed. Our bed. Our sacred place of comfort, canoodling, reading, and cherished moments of rest. Some seventy-five thousand hours of our lives together spent there. A nearby wall decorated with a Parisian scene in burnt umber. Chilewich flooring and floor-to-ceiling cream-colored drapes, every detail carefully selected when we built our dream house while our children were still in grade school. That place of peace on my side of the bed, where I routinely sat up to read while Amy took a hot bath in my line of vision in the bathroom due north through our walk-in closet.

I had dozed off for a bit, with Amy right next to me. When I opened my eyes, I sensed that she was very, very still. I gently put my hand on her chest and waited for a minute or two.

Then I slid out of bed, walked down the hall to our kids' room, and simply said, "It's over."

Amy was gone. Their mother, my wife, had succumbed to ovarian cancer.

After taking care of the details I knew were on my list when the time came, I went back to our room, gathered her lifeless body in my arms, and carried her down our stairs, through our dining room, and through our living room to a gurney that was waiting to take her away. Rigor mortis had kicked in. Her body weighed almost nothing, but it was stiff.

I was crying uncontrollably, so hard I was gasping for breath, when I let go of her, with loud, primal sounds that had never come out of me before.

The funeral home folks wheeled the gurney out of our house. I never saw her again.

In those first hours and days after Amy died, practical considerations inevitably took precedence over grief. She died on the thirteenth of March, and the kids and the family and I wanted a service as quickly as possible, so we set it for the fifteenth—not a great deal of time, obviously, to kick into gear and organize a proper memorial gathering.

Amy and I had had many talks after her ovarian cancer diagnosis was declared terminal. Among the topics of conversation were what she wanted done with her body and what kind of service she'd prefer. I can't emphasize strongly enough how important it is to work out these end-of-life details before the awful reality actually hits. Do it now, while you're still alive and (hopefully) well. Take it from me, when the time comes, it's impossible to think clearly. But because of our many conversations, the kids and the family and I weren't left with any guesswork at all.

What do you want done with your body? Amy wanted to be cremated.

Do you want your service at a religious venue, or a secular one? Give consideration to the generations that came before you. Would a religious venue give more comfort to the surviving parents and grandparents? And if you choose a church, or synagogue, or other religious facility, will they permit you to design the service you and your family want? Are they equipped to play music, and are they open to secular songs if that's what you choose? In our case, my best friend was president of a synagogue with a wonderful cantor to lead the service. She was very flexible and wide open to letting us design an occasion Amy would be proud of.

In the Jewish faith there is typically a period of mourning called shiva, where friends and family gather for a specific allotment of time, typically two to seven days (only for the very religious). I completely respect the practice. Amy, on the other hand, was fairly incredulous at the idea that someone dies and then everyone gathers at a family member's house to eat and drink. Having people descend on our home to eat and drink for days on end was not how she wanted to be remembered. We ended up striking what I still believe was a perfect balance between tradition and Amy's wishes—we had the shiva immediately following the service, at the temple where it was held. With the help of a lot of Amy's friends, our friends, the food and drinks, the decorations, the comfort level, the closeness, and the community in that room made it very respectful to Amy.

What about music at the service? Any specific preferences? Music had been such a huge—maybe even massive—part of our lives, so I made a list, of course, of songs I thought might work at the service. There were some no-brainers: the rock band Wilco, for sure, and not just because they were a Chicago-based hometown favorite. We'd also been to many, many Wilco shows together, from huge stages like Lollapalooza to more intimate settings like the Lyric Opera House and the Vic. So we played one of their songs, "Jesus, Etc.," at the service—yes, in a Jewish synagogue, but hey, this was all about Amy, right? Colin Hay's "I Just Don't Think I'll Get Over You" was too appropriate for me to pass up, with brilliant, haunting lyrics like "No longer moved to drink strong whiskey / I shook the hand of time and I knew / That if I lived till I could no longer climb my stairs / I just don't think I'll get over you." Our incredible cantor, who'd met with us in hospice and wanted Amy honored in true AKR style, sang a gorgeous rendition of Pearl Jam's "Just Breathe": "Stay with me. You're all I see." I still hear that song today and have to remind myself to "just breathe."

Believe it or not, shallow as it might sound, there was even a discussion about what the kids and I would wear to the service. I know, but it mattered to me to feel good about how I presented myself to the community, to the family, and to myself, if only to camouflage the utter and complete darkness I was drowning in emotionally. The four of us all made sure we had something really nice to wear that day, and it honestly did help.

One of the most important questions you'll want answers to in these end-of-life conversations is who should speak at the service. Amy and I gave this concept careful consideration. The hard part wasn't coming up with names, it was narrowing it down to just a few. We were blessed throughout our lives together with so many truly extraordinary, magical people we loved and who loved us, people who started out as friends, or nannies, or mannies, or assistants, or collaborators and came to be family.

Everyone we asked said yes, and everyone who spoke outside of the family gave me permission to share their words with you.

Hearing other people's words about Amy affected me in ways that, honestly, I never could have predicted. Of course, I'd known for years the effect that Amy had on people. Her gravity drew people in. Being a successful author meant that she had fans who loved and supported her work, so we often encountered people who would discuss the importance of her work to their lives or their kids' lives. But this was different. These people knew her, other sides of her being, encounters that I'd seen and heard of but only from her point of view. To see her like this, through so many different pairs of eyes, was a gift that, frankly, I never anticipated, but I cherish it more today than I ever could have imagined.

First there was Emily. Emily has the proud distinction of being our first connection to Appleton, Wisconsin. I am not sure what is in the water there, but clearly something we Rosenthals are drawn to. Emily will always hold a special place in our lives, not just for being such a wonderful human being with an infectious laugh but because she brought the sixth Rosie to us, our sweet and loyal dog Cougar. Emily started to work for Amy and our family when the kids were just six, eight, and ten. She stayed with us for two years.

Emily was Amy's assistant for one of the most exciting periods of time in her writing career. She assisted Amy with many facets of the extraordinary and unique memoir *Encyclopedia of an Ordinary Life*. Emily had a front-row seat to observe the unparalleled way Amy connected with her readers. She helped her mail pies to readers who responded to one of the challenges in Amy's book. She observed Amy's distinctive way of making meaningful connections with her readers, whether that was interacting with them online, via email, or with homemade treats.

Emily was quite young when she was with us and is now a proud mother of three herself. She credits her connection with Amy this way: "I can't imagine being the person, the wife, or the mother I am today without her. I will forever be grateful for the many ways she impacted my life," words she shared with the crowd that was gathered for Amy's memorial service. Of course, time spent with Amy meant one had to engage in certain activities no other boss would require. Emily also shared this anecdote: "It should also be noted that, being the same size as Amy, I got a kick out of the fact that she would send me to her tailor to try on her clothes for alterations." I know that memory will stay with Emily always.

Due to *Encyclopedia* being such a large part of Emily's life with our family, she ended her remarks with a favorite quote from that book:

> YOU
>
> Perhaps you think I didn't matter because I lived _____ years ago, and back then life wasn't as lifelike as it is to you now; that I didn't truly, fully, with all my senses, experience life as you are presently experiencing it, or think about _____ as you do, with such intensity and frequency.
>
> But I was here.
>
> And I did things.
>
> I shopped for groceries. I stubbed my toe. I danced at a party in college and my dress spun around. I hugged my mother and father and hoped they would never die. I pulled change from my pocket. I wrote my name with my finger on a cold,

fogged-up window. I used a dictionary. I had babies. I smelled
someone barbecuing down the street. I cried to exhaustion. I got
the hiccups. I grew breasts. I counted the tiles in my shower. I
hoped something would happen. I had my blood pressure taken.
I wrapped my leg around my husband's leg in bed. I was rude
when I shouldn't have been. I watched the celloist's bow go up and
down, and adored the music he made. I picked a scab. I wished I
was older. I wished I was younger. I loved my children. I loved
mayonnaise. I sucked my thumb. I chewed on a blade of grass.

I was here, you see, I was.

Nick, who was from Appleton and went to school with Emily's husband, spoke next. He came to us for an interview with shoulder-length unkempt hair, some sort of a lime green sweater, and an energy and enthusiasm the kids were drawn to immediately. It didn't hurt that he was willing to take them on in a game of basketball at his first interview. Nick became a manny for our family, starting in 2005, when the kids were eight, ten, and twelve years old.

The job was a combination of helping out with the kids and being Amy's assistant. As Nick described, "You see their laundry. How they snack. You see them on their off days." Little did we know that Nick had many hidden talents. Of significance was his musical prowess. That skill set not only endeared him to the kids but also became an entrée to a series of collaborations with Amy that included an amazing eighty-four pieces of music. Nick created original scores for a quite a few of Amy's films and songs for her books, conducted performance art experiences with Amy, and encouraged her to write some original pieces. He described working for Amy as being "like I'd won a lottery to be a wizard's apprentice."

And this wizard will display constant kindness, peerless
positivity, and will consistently err on the side of generosity
toward said apprentice. That is an actual thing. It's possible. I've
witnessed it. I experienced it.

Nick is a virtuoso on the piano, but he can also sing, play the mandolin, and compose music with the best of them. I would often hear Amy, as she stood at her computer, where she was known to work in our house, listening to clip after clip of some composition Nick had created for this or that project. Our family had the added bonus of appreciating Nick's creativity with a birthday song or video created just for the occasion. These were always silly and funny but also brilliant and original works of art. For his part, Nick talked to the crowd gathered for Amy's memorial service and discussed the unique nature of his working relationship with Amy:

What really set her apart as an art partner was that you got the
sense that she wanted to work with you because she was a fan
of yours. She loved you and wanted to make something cool
with you. She didn't hire you to be a cog. She wanted you to do
your thing. In that sense, she didn't treat you how she wanted to
be treated. She treated you how you *wanted to be treated. And*
therein, she wanted you to succeed.

As Nick concluded his remarks that day, the throngs that were gathered could hear Amy's voice begin to echo through the synagogue sound system, singing her and Nick's song "Wanna." I was the one who'd planned the service, so, of course, I'd known this was coming. Still, it was impossible not to be utterly devastated by the sound of her voice. But almost immediately everyone in the sanctuary was smiling through the tears as her incredible genius for wordplay winked at us through her lyrics:

> Wanna roast a marshmallow
> lightly charred
> Wanna rhyme this with
> Jean-Luc Godard
> Wanna be like a battery
> A total diehard but if my time is up
> I know I lived and loved hard

Nick shared with us the evolution of that song:

One of the last projects we collaborated on was a challenge that I issued to her last September. She had always been the initiator prior to this. I said, we should write a song together, Amy. You do the lyrics; I'll write the music. But you gotta sing it. She was hesitant about singing for fear of singing, but I said, if you don't sing, deal's off. A week later she had written five poems and was talking about doing an entire album!

As part of the creative process, Nick described an interaction they had after he presented some music to her as part of their collaboration. It is a microcosm of a typical AKR interaction. What Nick describes here is commonplace to anyone who had any sort of working relationship with Amy. That it came at the end of Amy's life is what makes this exchange worth including here. It says so much about Amy:

"Are you trying to score a movie? Is that harp? No. Sounds like pearly gates. None of that." I would have been insulted if she wasn't right and, also, it was just so badass. Even at the end, with a breathing tube and sapped of energy, artistic integrity and humor coursed through her veins, and she pushed me to a higher standard. Then and always.

To this day Nick has a special relationship with each of our kids, and he's part of a very close group that we now call family. He had a powerful impact on Amy's life. It was so moving to hear at the service that she had an equally powerful impact on his.

Then there was Ruby, who brought her intelligence, her humor, and her jack-of-all-trades skill set into our lives to help Amy through the completion of many, many projects and never missed a beat in the day-to-day responsibilities of working for a successful author. She was there throughout Amy's end-of-life struggles and watched her vitality slip away, but she did it with enormous poise and always kept her tears to herself as best she could. Ruby has a special place at the Rosenthal table and always will.

Ruby shared with us that she found the job on Craigslist. The copy for the job listing included free lunch, which appealed to Ruby immediately. Ruby did such an elegant job of sharing with us the depth of her relationship with Amy as a woman, an artist, a friend, a boss, and a mentor.

Amy wasn't just brilliant and creative. She had a true, raw love of her work. It is a palpable, contagious, precious thing she carried.

Amy seized on Ruby's brilliance and they collaborated on Amy's last memoir, *Textbook Amy Krouse Rosenthal*. There they would be, spending countless amounts of time debating a comma here or arguing over a semicolon versus ellipses there, and would pepper the house with pages from the book. But the biggest impact Ruby wanted to convey to those gathered for Amy that day was to share how much Amy meant to her as a person. Amy got to know Ruby so well, a side effect of working side by side with someone every day. She shared that Amy once wrote her a birthday card that said, "I hope today is filled with all your favorite things: Trees, friends, hummus, and crying." Each of these activities was illustrated in stick figure form. Of course, anyone who spends even a brief amount of time with Amy was gifted with her ingenious creativity:

> *Once, I showed up at work in a dreadfully sad mood. After attempting normal conversation for a bit, she gave up and sat down next to me. "Are you feeling a little purple today?" She explained that if a ruby were a bit blue, it would be purple.*

It is not difficult to see how Ruby remains a dear friend to our family. Her ongoing relationship with the kids will last a lifetime. And lucky for me, as I have embarked on a more creative version of myself, I have the good fortune of leaning on Ruby for all things relating to words and images.

Brian, a self-described "manny-slash–Marty Poppins," did such an extraordinary job in his eulogy of introducing himself and explaining why the kids and I consider him a Rosenthal for life. He, too, came from Appleton and was with our family from the time the kids were eleven, thirteen, and fifteen to sixteen, eighteen, and twenty. Consistent with what others shared about their time with Amy, Brian shared how Amy impacted his life:

> *She led by example. She showed me how to do the big things: practice kindness, be true to yourself—both as an artist and as a person—and what it takes to be an incredible parent and loving partner. And also the small, yet equally important stuff: How to admit a mistake. How to express gratitude. How to show you care about someone with a yellow Post-it note or loose-leaf homemade sign.*

Of course, the theme of Amy's enthusiasm for life was present in Brian's remarks as well. Sitting in the audience, overwhelmed with grief and barely able to hold my head up, I was filled with warmth hearing Brian talk about an average day with Amy.

> *I'd show up for work and she'd ask how my morning was. "Um, fine . . . I ate a peanut butter and banana sandwich." And she'd be like: "No way! They were just talking on NPR how Elvis ate a peanut butter and banana sandwich every morning. We should totally listen to Elvis this afternoon while we work."*

It was impossible not to smile through the tears listening to this very Amy moment. Like most things in her life, it was not the big moments that mattered. Instead it was times like this that made Amy the person we all think back on today.

It was our instinct to have these brilliant friends and collaborators talk with us about Amy's impact on their lives. When it came down to it, they each exceeded my expectations with their stories, their sincerity, and their humor. Oh, and did I mention that they *all* have Amy tattoos. Literally. I would challenge any group of former employees anywhere to see if their former employers made a permanent mark on their employees like Amy did here.

Several people asked me how I found the strength to speak at Amy's memorial service. The truth is, I couldn't imagine *not* speaking. Yes, I was devastated with grief; and yes, I was barely holding it together as I worked with my kids and family and friends and the synagogue staff on preparing for the day, our one chance to do it right. I just knew that I wanted everyone in that room to hear from me that Amy's impact on all our lives was every bit as incredible as she explained to the world in every word she wrote, everything she did, and every moment she lived.

I could never hope to be the wordsmith she was, but I did my best. I won't include the entire eulogy here, but I would like to offer one memory I shared with the audience that day:

> *Amy and I love live music. I would like to share a story with you that summarizes how playful and committed we were to our music. We were at a wedding downtown. But we had a serious conflict. One of our favorite bands was playing at Lollapalooza, which we had tickets for that weekend. Solution? We decided to do both. Amy brought her comfy shoes. During a break after the ceremony, we dipped out. Amy stashed her dress shoes in a planter outside and changed into her gym shoes. There we were. Running down Michigan Avenue. Formally dressed for*

*a wedding. I threw my tie around my head, wearing it like
a headband. We made the show! Soon we found ourselves
dashing back down the street, up the stairs to the wedding and
directly to the dance floor, as if we'd been there the entire time.
The bride danced over by us soon thereafter and, smiling, said
to Amy, "Oh, I am so glad someone else is sweating too, isn't
this great?" I think this encapsulates our joy for life together and
how we lived as a couple.*

I knew I had to share remarks about Amy that day. I could not let the chance to share a bit about our epic love story, include a bit about the impact of cancer and ask for a commitment to keep that disease in people's minds and emphasize Amy's impact on me and my life. Not long after, a friend sent a note about the service that read, "I'll remember it forever, and live my life differently because of it."

That's what Amy did for people, the imprint she left on their lives. When Amy entered your orbit, things forever changed. I know that better than anyone, because most of all, she did that for me.

PART III

Filling a Blank Space

11

Empty, Not Nest

Without clouds, there will be no rain;
without rain, trees cannot grow;
and without trees, we cannot make paper.

—*Thich Nhat Hanh*

You hear about it. You read about it. You see movies about it. You anticipate it over and over and over again, trying to brace yourself. But it turns out that nothing you do prepares you for the intensity of the emotional implosion that slams into you when your loved one takes her final breath.

It was more complicated than I'd expected. I knew I'd be decimated. I knew I'd be lonely, vulnerable, empty, and grief-stricken. I knew I'd be indescribably sad. Turns out that is pretty much accurate. And then some.

What I didn't know was how strongly I'd still feel Amy's presence at every turn and be brought to my knees by a song, a scent, a taste, walking past one of our favorite restaurants or just spotting a yellow . . . anything.

What I didn't know was how empty I would feel after two years of being singularly focused on her getting well; on being tuned in to her every minute of every day to make sure she was comfortable and in as little pain as possible; on thinking of every creative way I could come up with to remind her how loved she was—and now what? All that intense focus was suddenly gone, leaving no relief in its wake, just a hollow, gaping void and nothing to fill it with.

Most of all, though, what I didn't know, what I could only learn with time, and later in hindsight, was how much Amy's essay would become the backdrop for so much of my life following her death—both in those early days and long after. Suddenly I had the time to fully weigh the words that I'd struggled to process in the moment when the piece first came out. Of course, her writing had moved me and stirred up every emotion I'd had. But I hadn't dwelled on it because I was so focused on her and what we were going through together. I hadn't really thought of the implications of what she wanted for me. Of how she wanted me to use her death as an opportunity to continue to live my life. Of how this piece, written for all to see, was also a singular message to me.

Now that I had nothing but time to pore over her words, I found myself grasping the significance of what she wanted for me, of what she was trying to do. Reading her words, not just those from the essay but all the others that she had written in her career, left me with little pieces of her everywhere around me, each a clear reminder of how Amy had lived. Even though in the immediate aftermath, all I wanted to do was crawl into bed and stay there, I knew that was exactly what Amy wouldn't let me do.

More than anything, her words left me with the realization that whatever I chose to do with my blank space, I needed to make sure it was something I wanted. Amy had wanted me to make a plan. She'd wanted me to fill my blank space, to live my best life and make someone else happy. In theory I understood all that; in practice, I had no idea what any of it meant. After all, she knew me better than any person on the planet, so she knew I would struggle with how to go about filling that blank space she so publicly gave me. It almost seems like her list-making skills were put to the ultimate test as she left me pretty specific clues as to how to proceed forward.

Pick a moment in those first few months—honestly, they were all the same. There was no sunlight, only a few smiles, and certainly no laughter.

The early days were hazy at best—a collage of painful impressions with only a few specific events and faces. At worst they're just gone, days I don't remember that I never want back. At the beginning of April, just a few weeks after Amy's death, I decided to attend a previously scheduled work conference in DC. Not only are the entire two days lost to me now, but I felt that way immediately after I left the conference, as though all on its own my body had drifted there, occupied thinly cushioned chairs, been fed details about statutes and medical charts, and guided itself back to Chicago.

What does stand out for me about that time now is not so much a single person or event, but more the overwhelming feeling of love and support I experienced wherever I turned. The way in which people who mattered went out of their way to tell me what I meant to them—and how crucial that was to my beginning to feel like I could do this. My heart breaks for people who have to face similar trauma on their own. I don't know how I would have made it if that had been true for me.

Not surprisingly, it all started with family. The kids and I were surrounded and loved by our world-class family, and it still takes my breath away how they were, are, and always will be there for us, even when they were grieving the loss of their daughter, sister, daughter-in-law, and sister-in-law and dealing with challenges of their own.

During that awful time, my mom supported me in ways I never could have imagined. While she'd been there for me unconditionally all my life, she showed up without my even having to ask. She and Amy were so connected and shared so much together. Mom took Amy's death hard, but it never stopped her, not once, from being right there for me and her grandchildren whenever we needed her. She's youthful, fit, and still working. She lives near me in Chicago, so we're still physically connected as well and easily able to spend time together; and there's nothing we can't talk about, from finances to end-of-life issues to the grandchildren she adores. I've said it before, but it bears repeating—I credit my mother with making me the man I am today. All this care and support from Mom, mind you, while her husband, my stepfather, fell ill, lost his short-term memory, and had to be placed in a memory care facility, where he is to this day. My sister, Michel, was a supporting figure for me during this very dark time. A simple text, an offer of food, or a generous gesture like taking care of Cougar made it clear how much she cared.

I grew up the son of a therapist. My sister eventually got her degree in counseling psychology. My entire life I was surrounded by the reminders of "feelings," and how important it was to access them. It became almost a joke as I got older. I remember one Hanukkah my mom getting a gag gift. It was a psychotherapist doll that said on repeat, "And how did that make you feel?" With that upbringing, one would think that I had experience with psychoanalysis myself, but I had not.

My sister and my mom had encouraged me to seek out a good therapist while Amy was going through her illness, but I was not ready until after Amy died—I was simply too focused on her. Eventually, though, the point came when I knew I needed to work on myself to find a safe space to talk about issues I could not discuss with my family and kids. I wanted to talk about the complexities of being single, of single parenting, and of wanting to do something meaningful with my work life.

I found a good therapy match after a couple of stumbles, and can't imagine not having found that private time, even up to the current day.

And then there was my mother-in-law. Ann is like no other human I know on this planet. If you're looking for the cliché contentious son-in-law/mother-in-law relationship, don't waste your time looking here. Ann has made me feel like her son since the day I entered the Krouse family, and our connection has only deepened over the almost three decades we've been in each other's lives. She was there for almost every one of Amy's doctors' appointments, taking copious notes, asking the right questions, and holding Amy's hand. She was there for the most intimate caretaking moments of home hospice, and she never left the house without taking the time to assure me that everything I was doing for Amy was exactly the right way to approach the end of her life. She didn't need to be told how much I needed to hear it. She just knew.

She's been nothing but supportive and comforting since we lost Amy, and she continues to encourage me to keep telling my story. As difficult as it must be sometimes for her to hear me talk about her daughter, her work, her spirit, and our love story, Ann has been a smart, honest, enthusiastic sounding board for me and her grandchildren, no matter what we need to discuss. She even knows when to give advice and when to simply let us figure it out for ourselves. She also enjoys pointing out how ironic it is that she's Amy's mom because of their tremendously different approaches to fashion, fiction, and fun. Ann knows beyond a shadow of a doubt that everything about our relationship is reciprocal.

During long walks, lingering dinners, and extended visits, there's nothing we can't talk about, nothing off-limits or too personal, speaking openly and at length about life and death. A long walk in Atlanta, in her neighborhood in the suburbs of Chicago, or near her home in Florida would always result in an overall check-in about both of our lives. At one dinner in particular in Chicago, there we were, sharing how we each felt about our current lots in life. We have so much in common yet are a generation apart in our experiences of loss. Ann took that time to remind me how much it meant to her and my father-in-law that I took such great care of their daughter during the darkest time of all of our lives. I knew she meant it deep down in her heart, and hearing it truly made me feel a sense of reassurance that I'd done the right thing by taking care of Amy in home hospice. In our multilayered conversations, I tried to share my experience with the darkness of grief and, as she was experiencing her own loss, to reassure her that time itself does mysterious things, advice I received from others who had experienced intense loss.

Not to be outdone, every single one of our siblings, their spouses, and their children were extraordinary, the perfect combination of emotional connection, healthy space, and unconditional love in endless supply toward me and the kids. They all promised Amy that they would look after us, and they've kept that promise flawlessly, even while navigating the depth of their own loss. We shared so much joy as our kids were growing up together—the Sunday gatherings, the Shabbat dinners, the family trips, celebrating large and small milestones, just hanging out. That we could share sorrow with the same loving, unedited closeness is a gift I'll never take for granted.

My in-laws lived for years in a home built for family. We often had family dinners there, sometimes all twenty-three of us, sitting around laughing and eating and sharing stories. Each and every dinner started with a toast from our patriarch, Amy's dad, Paul. This tradition carried on after Amy died, even if the table was not quite full of all of our family members (kids in other cities working, or off to college). I remember clearly one such dinner in June 2017. There we were, cousins ranging in age from two to twenty-four, going around the table and sharing stories. I was in my new "crying" phase, where I could not get through talking about Amy without shedding a tear. The sense of family was deep. The love in the room radiated, a feeling I am so grateful for—one I know many people are not so lucky to have.

Of course, family isn't always blood; and leading the pack of close, true friends who were there to see the kids and me through the darkest times and walk me toward the light again were Jeff and Dave, who've been my sidekicks for over fifty years.

I met Jeff in a parochial nursery school in Chicago. Dave made his entrance a year later, in kindergarten. We have been best friends ever since. Dave was my best man at Amy's and my

wedding, and Jeff was the contractor when Amy and I built our dream house. Our wives became friends and shared mad mutual respect. Jeff's wife became one of Amy's closest friends, and our daughters are close in age and have a special bond. Dave's son is very much my nephew. Over our five decades together, "my boys" and I have been through births, bar mitzvahs, wins and losses, successes and failures, marriages, and, ultimately, loss together. The support I felt and continue to feel from these two guys and their families is difficult to describe, beyond saying that they were and are just there for me, plain and simple, and it means everything.

The three of us know that we can say anything to one another with zero judgment. Over the course of our lives, that has morphed from childhood silliness to girls in high school to issues relating to long-term marriages and raising children. After

I lost Amy, they found ways to connect with me on a deeper level, whether that was more meaningful phone conversations about how I was feeling—yes, guys do have the capacity to talk about emotions—or spontaneous texts about a moment that reminded them of Amy. These guys, along with several other of my good friends, were excellent at distracting me as well. Our tradition of seeing our favorite blues artist, our childhood friend Dave Specter, became a welcome distraction from the depths of grief. This process was new for all of us, and even though they too were grieving the loss of their dear friend, they figured out how to be there in a perfect way for me.

This quote from a *Friends* episode takes on new meaning for me as I think about all of these guys: "Friends don't let friends suffer from jellyfish stings."

And then there were the kids.

They were on my mind every minute, and I was frightened. Not about them. They're amazing young adults, and I'm so proud of them. They'd been Herculean every step of the way, from their mom's initial diagnosis to her death to her memorial service. They comforted me every bit as much as I comforted them.

No, what I was frightened about was my ability to be a single parent.

Amy and I had countless conversations about this very topic in her final weeks. It is one of the gifts I feel I received from having the time to be with her at the end stage of her life. Not everyone is as fortunate—if the loss is sudden and unexpected, for example. In those super-intimate moments, I would ask Amy how I could be the best parent in her absence. How could I handle the milestones and the spaces in between? Amy would think about it long and hard and then say with confidence, "You are an amazing dad. You have such a special relationship with each one of the kids. You don't need to think too hard about it. They love and respect you." She emphasized that I "could do it." Honestly, I am unsure if I could have without her clear affirmation that we all would be okay. Still, Amy was so incredibly gifted at having that "mother wit." As dudes, we sometimes just don't get it.

That is not meant to be a sexist statement. I feel as if I was incredibly involved and competent at a lot of child-rearing issues. But there's something special, even irreplaceable, about a mother-child relationship. Period. There were college graduations coming up. I was destroyed, imagining trying to plan the right celebrations, and counsel and guide our kids through career decisions and job searches. Weddings? Come on. How could Amy not be here for those? How could I navigate them alone? Amy always knew what to say, when to hug, when to give space, when to be firm, and when to simply love like only a mother can. Now she was gone, and I was still here, feeling like I could never begin to make up the difference.

My first major single-parenting test arrived when my son Miles's graduation came along in May 2017. We were going to Atlanta for the graduation. Now, there was no typical AKR list to follow. All of the details were on me. It is not that this was a hard thing to pull together, but I was not used to having all of this fall on me. Booking flights and hotels. Making fun dinner reservations. Writing creative cards, planning a good toast— okay, that was my specialty—and bringing together my mother-in-law and my mom.

Amy had some forethought here as well. Our family has a tradition of making signs and posting them all over the kitchen at significant moments in our lives, big and small. Examples include birthdays, welcome-home signs, first and last day of school, and so forth. In her final months, she made signs for Miles's graduation. I brought them with me. They were not the typical witty, word-punny sorts that Amy usually made, but the significance of the moment was clear. This added an entirely different layer of emotion to an already sentimental affair.

In the end, the weekend was a mixture of this overwhelming emotion and the culmination of four intense years for our middle child. Not many kids his age had to struggle with the hardship of losing a parent while staying on course to get a well-earned degree in a complex subject. Mixed in with the sadness of Amy's absence were moments of pure joy and pride as I watched my son receive his diploma in his cap and gown.

Miles's graduation was difficult in so many ways, but it wasn't until it was over that the bottom really dropped out. That was when I started having panic attacks.

I would have random periods in the day when my heart started to beat in a forceful way that caused me to struggle to catch my breath. The first time it happened, I thought it was something physical, as in a cardiac issue. I do not have a specific memory of an exact trigger that brought on this feeling, but I mention it because after a major loss you have to expect the unexpected, both physically and emotionally. So much of this new life was a presentation of unexpected experiences and challenges. There was a gap in my heart, in my bed, and in my thoughts.

When it started to occur more frequently, never at the same time of day, I talked to my therapist about it. I remember clearly sitting on her couch and having the feeling come up in her office. By then, I thought I was having some anxiety. I wondered if this was a normal reaction to grief. She assured me that many emotional responses manifest themselves in physical characteristics. She did, however, encourage me to see my doctor.

And that's how I found myself in my doctor's office on May 11, 2017, taking a stress test. Be careful what you say to your doctor. He had no choice but to order the test. I got wired up and did my turn on the treadmill. I passed with flying colors. The mere comfort of knowing I was not having a heart attack surely made the symptoms recede. I did not have another incident.

Still, the episode lingered in its own way. It marked the first time I truly understood just how complicated and profound the layers surrounding loss can be, not just our internal responses but our bodies' behaviors as well. This revelation was an incredibly powerful one: loss has emotional and physical components that one has no control over. To successfully navigate this new landscape, I would have to understand that—the sooner, the better.

12

Refueling Mind and Body

Life is strange. You keep moving and keep moving. Before you know it, you look back and think, "What was that?"

—*Joe Rogan*

The panic attacks were eye-opening on so many levels, and perhaps chief among them was the realization that before I could do anything else with my life, I had to start taking better care of myself.

For the two years I was taking care of Amy, and for months after she died, I wasn't taking care of myself. I thought I was, but in truth, I'd lost a lot of weight, stopped exercising, and generally wasn't caring for myself. Health, wellness, nutrition, and exercise had been major priorities for Amy and me throughout our marriage, and we passed those priorities along to our children.

It's never been in me to sit back with my feet up and wait for things to happen. It's my nature to be active, to be a participant and appreciate that I have been born into a certain privilege in this world, but also that I have to earn my place in it. Almost to try to reconnect with that man Amy married, the man I'd lost track of, I did what she would have done and made a list of the jobs I'd gone out and found from the time I was a boy:

Age 8—Newspaper route

Age 11—Neighborhood hardware store

Age 13—Neighborhood pharmacy

High school—Health club/photography business entrepreneur/ production assistant/movie theater/law office clerk

College—Short-order cook/window washer/assistant to member of Parliament

Law school—Bartender/law clerk

I was ready to dive back into being a participant again.

Starting therapy had been a crucial first step.

Then, knowing perfectly well from many years of experience that yoga makes differences that only start with the body, I headed to a yoga studio near my house, where I took up a method of exercise called "sculpt." It's a combination of weights, yoga, and cardio, and I was drawn to it because of its intensity and its connection to yoga. I had heard how difficult the classes were, and wanted to try it out. The workout was like nothing I had ever experienced—super intense, very sweaty, and, with the right teacher, a very inspiring hour and a half.

Amy, by the way, would have hated it, not because of the intensity of the workout but because she HATED group exercise. That is why we did ashtanga yoga for many years—it has a set series of poses that never change no matter where you are in the world, and it can be done in private or a group setting. If I was to do a spinning class, or any other group class, she would encourage me. But the beat of loud music, all of it, made her cringe; and the mere suggestion from the teacher to "Keep it up, you can do it!" or "You are strong, you can do anything if you put your mind to it!" made her absolutely crazy.

In this case, the sculpt instructor was a lovely soul I connected with because of her spiritual approach to our sessions. She talked a lot about "setting an intention" to the practice. I'd heard that before, more than once, and always thought, "Yeah, my intention is to work my butt off and get a good sweat." "Setting an intention" sounded a little woo-woo to me, and I found it difficult to resonate with. But now I found myself interpreting "setting an intention" in a whole new way, something along the lines of "Embrace this new life," or "Think more about love and less about anger over my loss." An intention can range from being grateful or feeling peaceful to something more physical, such as focusing on breath or working through an injury. Typically, the teacher asks us to set an intention at the beginning of the class and refer back to it at the end in some capacity. The intention I would set varied from day to day. Sometimes I literally could not embrace the concept, and on other days I felt so connected to it. As I made this rigorous practice more of my regular routine, I warmed up to the intention-setting concept as a spiritual connection to the physical work.

It helped. A lot. So much so that before long I started incorporating Pilates and functional physical fitness into my normal routine. The physical challenge was intense and felt wonderful. The emotional self-connection and release felt even better.

I'd done some meditation before, and I'm sure there will be some eye-rolling out there by some of you who read this and think I'm wandering into fad territory; but the truth is that taking up the daily practice of meditating has changed my life. I'd already done some reading about thought leaders, successful business owners, and fitness gurus extolling the benefits of meditation. When I committed to making a habit of it on my own, I read more about the neuroscientific advantages, and about different teachers and practitioners, and meditating went from being kind of a cool thing to do to being a logical, vital, healing thing to do. Before long, and to this day, the simple act of sitting still for ten minutes every morning has opened my eyes to being mindful of my internal and external worlds.

I wasn't drawn to the idea of a therapeutic group setting to help me through losing Amy. Something about it felt forced to me. Don't get me wrong; I am well aware that group therapy has proven extremely rewarding and successful to many people who experience profound loss. I am an introvert by nature, however, and I just felt like my process could come more effectively from individual therapy and from my network of family and friends.

Within the first few weeks of Amy's death, a dear friend introduced me to Sheryl Sandberg, with whom she had been working on a project. In the course of their conversations, Amy's article came up, and of course Sheryl had read it. I have to plead ignorance here—I did not know much about Sheryl. Looking back now, that seems crazy. I was vaguely familiar with her story of loss but had to refresh my memory. Soon she sent me an advanced copy of a book she'd written with Adam Grant that was about to be published, a book called *Option B: Facing Adversity, Building Resilience, and Finding Joy*. It became a kind of guidebook for me; so many of the stories contained in it resonated deeply. While our versions of loss—sudden vs. slow onset—were very different, I immediately felt a real kismet with her. Seeing my new experiences in print, as part of a shared story, was so comforting. I owe a huge debt of gratitude to her, and since then I have modeled the generous behavior she showed me with others in my life who have faced unbearable loss.

Gradually, as my radar went up again and other people's stories came into my awareness, I began to dip into the lives of other widowers and those who experienced profound loss as I had. Digesting these incredible stories made me feel like I was developing my own version of a grief group. Snippets of other people's experiences of loss connected with me deeply. There was also something comforting in not having to engage with someone in intimate conversation but instead being able to process the connection in my own way. It was part of my "work," and ultimately encouraged me to tell my own story. It turns out that even though everyone experiences loss differently, there's enormous comfort and hope in learning how other widows and widowers (Isn't that the oddest word, by the way? It kind of sounds like "one who widows") got through the inevitable painful darkness, and *that* they got through it.

Because it is now an ingrained Rosenthal trait, here's a list of the books I strongly recommend if you're struggling through this journey yourself:

Option B: Facing Adversity, Building Resilience, and Finding Joy, by Sheryl Sandberg and Adam Grant

The Widower's Notebook, by Jonathan Santlofer

The Light of the World, by Elizabeth Alexander

When Breath Becomes Air, by Paul Kalanithi

The Iceberg, by Marion Coutts

Young Widower, by John W. Evans

Living with the End in Mind, by Erin Tierney Kramp and Douglas H. Kramp

In a Dark Wood, by Joseph Luzzi

*You Are Not Alone: A Heartfelt Guide for Grief, Healing, and
Hope*, by Debbie Augenthaler

Gratitude, by Oliver Sacks

The Art of Losing, by Kevin Young

*What to Do When I'm Gone: A Mother's Wisdom to Her
Daughter*, by Suzy Hopkins and Hallie Bateman

*The Five Innovations: Discovering What Death Can Teach Us
about Living Fully*, by Frank Ostaseski

The Bright Hour: A Memoir of Living and Dying, by Nina Riggs

The Missing Piece, by Shel Silverstein

This Is a Poem That Heals Fish, by Jean-Pierre Siméon

Cry, Heart, but Never Break, by Glenn Ringtved

Michael Rosen's Sad Book, by Michael Rosen

Of course, reading, helpful as it was, would get me only so
far. Learning how others have struggled with grief was powerful and poignant, but it also reminded me that learning was
only one piece of this story. The time I was spending on myself
was hugely important—I felt my energy returning slowly but
surely, I spent less time in bed—and these changes opened up
more emotional space for me to begin thinking more concretely
about my new life and how I was going to fill that proverbial
blank space.

The panic attacks were scary, difficult to overcome in so
many ways, but in their aftermath, I began to emerge the better
for them. Week by week, I began to feel like I would be able to
get through this—something that I hadn't been sure of just a
month earlier.

But the further I crawled out, the more questions began to

flood in. The immense sense of loss and sadness that I felt in the wake of Amy's death was debilitating, but it was also liberating in a way; I felt no pressure, no need to think about any other part of myself than grief. As I stepped tentatively back into the world, suddenly I had questions to answer, decisions to make. Not just about immediate issues like what to have for dinner, what shirt to wear, but big-picture stuff—about not only my present but my future as well.

And in those moments I found myself thinking more and more about that blank space at the end of Amy's *New York Times* essay and accepting it as a gift, an unrestricted endowment from her, not just her permission but her blessing to fill it with new chapters of my life.

Perhaps I shouldn't have been surprised when, just as I thought I had the beginnings of my plan figured out, life intervened.

13

Navigating a Maze of Emotions

One day we'll all be ghosts
Tripping around in someone else's home.
One day we'll all be ghosts, ghosts, ghosts,
Ghosts, ghosts, ghosts.

—*The Head and the Heart*

It was July 26, 2017, when I got the call that my dad, Arnie, had passed away.

It wasn't a complete shock. Throughout my adult life my relationship with him was mostly as his caretaker; he suffered from Parkinson's disease for many, many years and was fortunate enough to spend his last years in an assisted living facility. Still, it was brutal watching this once vibrant and cool man, with more than his share of hair and girlfriends, in a long decline. Visiting him was a chore. He was able to give so little emotionally, and his inclination was to complain. About anything and everything. What finally took Dad's life was dysphagia, a severely compromised ability to swallow, apparently not uncommon as Parkinson's disease progresses.

My experience of losing my dad was a bit conflicted. On one hand, just a few months after losing Amy, it was painful to be plunged headfirst back into grief. Just as I thought I was going in a better direction, I had to confront feelings of loss all over again. On the other hand, though, to be completely honest, I was at peace with his passing. He'd been living a very, very difficult life, and he'd never seemed happy. His physical limitations had become so extreme that it was impossible for him to enjoy the simple pleasures of everyday life—going to a diner for a chocolate phosphate, for example, or his weekly outings with his brother Howard for a hot dog.

I was relieved for him that he was free of a body and mind that were making him so miserable. I was relieved for me that I'd been freed from the burden of continuing to be his caretaker; after the long time I'd spent caring for Amy, simply put, I was exhausted. But as with grief in general, the impact of losing my father wove its way in and out of my consciousness and made the emotional process that much more difficult to navigate.

In the end, my father's death carried an emotional toll all its own—albeit not one that I could have fully predicted. While I obviously grieved for my father, his death made me feel Amy's absence even more acutely. Amy had always been there for me when it came to him—or to life in general, for that matter—and this was the first loss I'd suffered since her passing. In the aftermath of my father's death, I was reminded of how immediately Amy and I understood our respective struggles and the unspoken agreement between us that whatever those struggles were, we'd get through them together.

Not many people understood my challenges with my father in the same way Amy did, without my ever having to explain it to her, or even say a word about it unless I just needed to. The complexities of my relationship with him were not lost on her.

She was there when I returned from a visit with him and had to unwind by venting to her.

"Did he ask you one question about you?" she'd ask, even though she already knew the answer. I was usually a sounding board for all of the things Arnie found to complain about. Amy would listen to me repeat his list of things that were wrong in his life: the institutional food, his lack of training to use a computer so he could finish his book, the allegedly rough way he was handled by the staff, and on and on.

Amy and I would put things in perspective together. We would remind Dad that he was beyond fortunate to live where he did at no cost to himself; that his sons were there financially if he needed anything; that his kids schlepped him to countless doctors' visits; that his brother was there religiously to take him out for his regular hot-dog excursions; and that he had incredible grandkids with whom he could develop relationships. Amy had her own unique way of bringing me back to reality after a visit with him, of making me feel like a good son, and of helping me simply get used to the fact that I would not get anything in return from this complex relationship.

Now suddenly I had to confront this maze of emotions on my own, without Amy to lean on. It was humbling to realize how empty I still felt, even after months of what I'd told myself was progress. Above all else, though, it was just incredibly sad.

Perhaps nothing crystallized my fraught emotions more than sitting down to prepare my remarks for my dad's funeral. As I tried to think of the right words, I was overcome with a feeling of profound certainty—Amy would have known what to say. But not just that, she would have helped me figure out what

I wanted to say. Instead, I had to figure it out on my own. And just that fact—that I'd lost my sounding board, my friend who was there to help me deal with moments precisely like this— left me at a loss for words, not just about my father, but about everything.

Thankfully, just when I'd almost given up on finding much of anything to talk about but my struggles with Dad, my high school prom date texted me out of the blue and shared some wonderful memories of him, even though their encounter had been brief. As with many challenges I would come to face, I started to think about him from a place of being grateful for what he stood for in my life. My dad was, after all, a very ac- complished artist, a jazz drummer, and a historian, and he had a wealth of idiosyncrasies, including his love of Fanta grape soda, chocolate phosphates, and hot-dog gum. In the end, I was able to eulogize him in a way that showed respect for the man he'd been in my life.

As Arnie's death threw me back into my grief for Amy, something unexpected happened, purely by chance, that went a long way to helping me focus on my blank space: Miles, who had recently graduated from college in Atlanta, came home to Chicago and moved back in with me.

Now this wasn't anyone's "idea," it just sort of happened in the way that lots of kids move home after college graduation. Miles had his own plans for his future, and home seemed like a good place to put things in motion. The timing could not have been more perfect.

Of course neither of us knew at the outset what it would be like living together without Amy, but as it turned out, the match was great. Each of us provided something for the other at that unspeakably difficult time. For me, the sight of my middle child emerging from his childhood bedroom felt so comforting, a sense of normalcy in a period when nothing felt normal. *Oh, there's Miles coming out of his red room, right where he belongs.*

It became clear early on that we were entering a new phase of our relationship, though. My days of fathering a young boy were over. Sure, I had a lot of anxiety about single parenting. Those concerns frequently crept in, but mostly our relationship was redefining itself. I soon began a new life as a single person, and Miles was right there with a window into my new life. Sometimes that would mean I was out late. Other times it meant a traditional "Dad dinner," something I knew Miles deeply appreciated.

But it was the in-between moments that brought us that much closer. Whether that came in the form of pausing in the morning before work for a good conversation about an article or current events, or diving deep into exchanging thoughts about a podcast we'd heard, I saw with such clarity that this was not just my son and my new roommate but a grown-up man processing his own grief.

We continued our tradition of cooking meals together and trying out new restaurants. We frequented neighborhood joints. We talked about books, and he introduced me to some great nonfiction I would never have known about without him. We explored the new territory of family gatherings and social events together without Amy and learned to enjoy them, and we traveled to a wedding as a team. Having Miles in my life in this intimate way took some of the sting out of the loss I'd been struggling with.

The fact that this happened after my father's death, after I'd felt that profound sense of Amy's absence all over again, was not lost on me. My father's death had been a step back for me, and having a new support in place made a huge difference. There were times when I felt so sad and vulnerable to my darkest possible emotions, and then Miles would be there. Likewise, there were other times when I saw Miles and felt so incredibly grateful that I could still look forward to being a father to three outstanding human beings. Just being near him helped renew my sense of purpose; for the first time in months, I found myself living not just day to day but with *intention*.

Whatever I did with my blank space, whatever my plan would be, my kids would be my bedrock. The combination of Arnie's death and living with Miles helped me realize just how much of my future needed to be spent appreciating what I had, not dwelling on what I'd lost. My father had given up so much by not being a more active part of my life. And now, unlike my dad, I'd had the privilege of being with my wife, raising our three amazing kids together, knowing them inside and out, watching them grow into extraordinary young adults, sharing everything from adventures all over the world to boring chores and homework. I wonder if Arnie ever thought about those lost moments with Michel and me.

In a leap of courage, I asked Miles to step in here for a moment and write whatever he wanted to say about the impact of this past couple of years on him. I didn't have to tell him to be honest. I knew he would. But I wasn't prepared for this:

There are too many important memories to capture in a single spouting of memories, too many defining moments that are embedded and tethered together in my family's collective consciousness. In the midst of the most defining, tragic period of our lives, joy found its subtle way to emerge. In late February of 2017, my family and I were tending to my mother as she lived out her final hospice days in the comfort of our home, my childhood nest. The seclusion we had was important, away from the semi-publicity and chaos of a hospital, we were confined to our space of preeminent choice in any circumstance; we were close to each other and to our matriarch, the one who was somehow chosen to deal with the most acute and painful of burdens, the emperor of all maladies. During this time, I was working to finish my spring and final semester of college. This also entailed searching for a post-graduation job for the period after this terrible personal event would be reduced to memories.

Within the last few weeks of my mom's life, I received an acceptance call from what would be my future employer— this onerous task was over. What was worth some mild celebration was that the job would be in Chicago, and that unequivocally meant moving back in to live and be with my dad. My mom was too sick to feel excited, but I was elated to tell Dad. Strangely and obviously, I remember the joy I felt during that afternoon when sharing the news; it was enough to temporarily drown out, or really dampen, the pain and terror of the imminence of my mom's death. Shortly after this episode, we reached the apotheosis of the dark of the night, and my mother would finally leave this world, and us. There was no way back. However much gloom and fog made it difficult to see, there was a way forward. For me, 80% of that was called Dad.

At work, it was clear early on that I would have to put double the effort in in order to release myself of the pull towards, and being consumed by, thoughts of my mom, while also learning the plethora of new things that a first job requires. There was a considerable amount of time throughout the hospice stage where I thought that when it all became the past, it would be far more manageable than living with only the memories. I would come to no longer believe in the truth of this ideal; the density of it all was just too great. What offered some incredible recompense, however, was merely being in my dad's presence and even more so the graciousness and generosity he showed and gave me without ever asking for anything in return. Upon walking through the revolving door of my office building and into the evening, hearing the cacophony of downtown Chicago noises, I most looked forward to getting off the "L" and re-entering my old home where my dad would often be waiting for me. If I was particularly lucky, I'd open that mighty wooden front-door and step into a house filled with the intoxicating scents of garlic, butter, and rosemary as he concocted a small masterpiece. While I was in my childhood home, it was also blatantly obvious how different everything truly was. At our home, there was always something close enough to bite and remind me of the presence that was there but wasn't.

My dad spent a lot of time focused on learning about the ways that individuals and cultures respond to grief, consuming books on the subject from as wide an array of authors as possible; they would pile high in the corner of his room, on his nightstand, and on the dining room table he gradually

transformed into a second office. In recent years, my dad has
provided the world the opportunity to hear his words and
consume this knowledge and the profundity of both his ideas
and messages, and the responses they have been strong—people
are moved, and they are thankful. Nothing about my dad has
fundamentally changed since my mom's death and throughout
our 700-or-so days of cohabitation. He is still gentle and kind,
strong of mind and body, generous and shrewd, creative,
pensive and composed, and mostly, for me and my siblings, the
embodiment of a father in its best sense. Many seek to learn
from him, and many will continue to.

I have been lucky enough to be in such close proximity
to him as to witness and receive the enactment of the
aforementioned qualities, and I will always remember it as a
time filled with immense love and appreciation. I could have
chosen to break from my family, my city and my home in order
to create a new life away from the terrors of the past, but it
was only through returning home and living alongside that
great man that I was able to feel connected to and nurtured
by the part of him that I came to understand truly embodied
my parents and my mother. I have found nothing in my brief
sojourn on Earth that imbues me with as much a sense of
completeness as being with my father. I owe him more than I
could ever hope to repay, but it's a testament to the man he is
that he may very well say the same exact thing about me.

Of all the profound lessons that living with Miles afforded
me, perhaps the most powerful was that it lessened the fears
that had been plaguing me since even before Amy's death about
my ability to parent my kids on my own. Yes, a mother/child

relationship is unique and irreplaceable. But so is a father/child relationship, if you give it the best you've got and don't leave the "emotional intimacy" part to the mom because you assume women are better at it.

Living with Miles in such proximity reinforced something that I'd known theoretically but hadn't been able to truly experience since Amy's death: parenting on my own was indeed different, but I was up for the challenge. Miles and I became closer than ever, and the best part was that it wasn't just me watching him grow anymore. He started to watch me grow as well. As we wandered through the grief of losing Amy together, we held each other up every step of the way as no one else could have, giving each other plenty of support and freedom to process the new lives stretching out ahead of us, one blank space at a time.

14

The Heal Jason Tour

God has given us music so that above all it can lead us upwards. Music unites all qualities: it can exalt us, divert us, cheer us up, or break the hardest of hearts with the softest of its melancholy tones. But its principal task is to lead our thoughts to higher things, to elevate, even to make us tremble.... The musical art often speaks in sounds more penetrating than the words of poetry, and takes hold of the most hidden crevices of the heart.... Song elevates our being and leads us to the good and the true.

—*Friedrich Nietzsche*

While living with Miles afforded me a stability I never could have imagined, I was still prone to my share of rough patches, still trying to reconnect with that guy I'd always been, that guy who felt happy, curious, and enthusiastic about life.

One of the most challenging aspects of this time in my life was my chosen career as a lawyer. Over the years, Amy and I had talked so often about my finding a bit more meaning, even joy, in my professional life. I knew that trying to emulate Amy's level of utter joy and commitment to her work, though she never considered what she did for a living as "work" in the technical sense, was impossible. At the same time, I was forced to think about the ultimate pivot. Unfortunately, it sometimes takes a profound event like the one I was faced with to really deeply consider what purpose work has in this life. That certainly was the case for me.

I'd been self-employed ever since the kids were little, which provided me the freedom to be the family man I wanted to be and was. However, this moment in time caused me to really reflect on the day-to-day insignificance of what I had been doing. Did I want to haggle with insurance adjusters? Hell, no. Was financial comfort all that was left of being a solo practitioner? Administrative obligations overwhelmed the actual practice of law. This was not a path that I wanted to continue on for long. My entire life's focus had changed, and my law career compounded my lack of clarity instead of bringing things into focus.

My presence at my law office diminished quickly. As I began to take better care of myself, I did not beat myself up if I went to yoga in the morning instead of rushing to work. If I was in the throes of a good book, I might keep reading for a bit before feeling that draw, that need to be in the office at a certain time, that plagued me most of my adult life. Even to this day, I am unable to completely shut my doors at the firm, still dealing with the idea of closing off a part of my identity. But as the days go on and I continue to focus on what is meaningful in my life, the practice of law, such as it is, has moved to the bottom rung of the ladder. Mindfulness, meditation, yoga, music, family, and friends have guided me to think about new ways to contribute in this life. It is a work in progress.

And in many ways, having Miles around reinforced the need to start doing new things even more. Because his presence was such a welcome change, it helped me think about what could happen if I began to make other changes. I could see clearly now, for the first time in months, that I was in serious need of a place where I could figure out how to be myself again.

Not surprisingly, my thoughts drifted back to places Amy and I had traveled, in particular on our honeymoon. California and Colorado. Big Sur, and the mountains. We'd loved it there. Majestic, exhilarating, brand-new air with every breath, life everywhere. The more I thought about it, the more it felt like the perfect place to rejuvenate. Though to some it might seem difficult to revisit a place so integral to my life with Amy, I wasn't worried about going there by myself and feeling her presence all around me. That was already happening no matter where I was, so I might as well let it happen in a couple of the most beautiful places I'd ever seen.

I ran the idea past Miles, who thought it was a great idea. Then he casually added, "Why don't you do something you would never have done with Mom?"

His words stopped me in my tracks: what a simple, powerful idea. I would never have thought of it. This boy always was wise beyond his years.

For starters, I did some research that night and found out that one of my favorite bands, Tedeschi Trucks Band, was scheduled for an upcoming gig at the Red Rocks Amphitheater, ten miles west of Denver, famous for being, among other things, the world's only naturally occurring acoustically perfect amphitheater. Yes, please.

Then, under the heading "Something you would never have done with Mom," I tossed out an invitation to my crew of friends to meet me in Colorado for the Red Rocks show. I hadn't done a "boys' trip" during my twenty-six years of marriage, preferring to be with Amy if we had any time to travel together. Why not now?

Much to my delight, five of the guys said yes, and we were off.

From the first hour we were together, I knew this decision was just what I needed. The concert itself was spectacular—an amazing show in an amphitheater you have to see to believe. It's built into a rock structure, with a large disc-shaped rock forming a backdrop for the stage and huge rocks framing the stage, so that the almost ten thousand people in the audience feel as if they're cradled in the most unparalleled beauty nature has to offer.

More powerful than the setting, though, was the fact that every one of those friends stepped up to encourage me to just relax and have fun, without a moment of guilt or judgment if I had an extra tequila, or let go with a long, cathartic laugh, or stood up and danced. It was the first time in a while that I didn't feel as much like a widower as I just felt like Jason, hanging out with some old pals who knew me and wanted nothing but the best for me. I hadn't realized how much I needed it until I was in the middle of it, felt myself taking long breaths of fresh air, and heard myself really laughing without wondering if it was too soon for it to be appropriate.

Of course, my thoughts would always drift back to Amy, but instead of getting swept up in them, I was able to acknowledge them without losing myself. The day of the concert, we were wandering around the quaint, tiny town of Morrison, Colorado, home of the Red Rocks Amphitheater, and happened to stroll into a tchotchke shop to browse around. I did a double take when I glanced at a display and saw this tile:

new life
chapter one

Was it serendipity? A sign? An affirmation from Amy some-how that this was all okay? Even if it was none of the above and I was reading something into pure coincidence, you can bet I bought that tile and brought it home.

I found out later that my friend Michael called the trip "the Heal Jason Tour," and in a lot of ways, he was exactly right. I still had a long way to go—there's definitely no timetable for grief and all of its complexities. But it was a huge step in the right direction. Time out with great friends, a major change of scenery, and a thrilling infusion of live music were enough to reignite my pilot light.

As my plane touched down in Chicago, I instantly recognized the impact that the trip had had on me. Not only was I proud of myself for having initiated it in the first place, I remembered all at once just how transformative leaving home can be. I promised myself I'd say yes to every possible new opportunity and let travel and music help give me the emotional nourishment I'd been missing for a long time.

After the Heal Jason Tour, the floodgates opened, and I soaked it all in. I went on a ski trip with a college buddy, where I hung out with a bunch of great guys I had never met before. Justin, Miles, and I accepted an invitation from a dear friend to his secluded home in Montana. I had been to this idyllic spot before and was aware of its healing power. I also knew that these friends made things so easy and exerted no pressure on me. There was something about that place in nature that provided serenity of mind and body. Merely sitting and watching a stream roll by, hearing the beautiful sound of flowing water, made me grateful to be there in that time and place, to appreciate what was in front of me—literally, and in the sense of how essential it was to appreciate this life and the short time we all have in it, as well as to follow Amy's edict that I must go on.

Perhaps most affecting and important, the kids and I went on a wonderful excursion a few months later, in December. Planning this trip for the four of us came with mixed emotions. The last big adventure I'd planned for our family, for the five of us, had to be canceled due to Amy's inability to travel. But we had a rich history of annual family trips that always included some time to be just us Rosies, and I sensed that we needed a return to this comfort, to peel away from the everyday, from the rest of the world, no one else, only us.

This was our first trip without Amy, and I was not sure how things would shake out. I was confident that all of the kids wanted to do this, to be together. I was aware that they were all incredible travelers, adventurous because we'd exposed them to travel from an early age. This was new territory, however, for all of us.

Many of the experiences we shared on this wonderful trip felt natural, like we were meant to be there together. We had fun, we did things we could not do at home (a camel ride, walking the tightly woven streets, visiting old synagogues), and we made new memories.

We were good at talking about Amy by now, but this time of reflection allowed us to check in with one another and see how we were all doing, individually and as a group. We freely and easily talked about their mom, and we laughed a lot, but there were tears as well, of course. I was the only one who got really ill on this trip. But I pressed through, realizing the beauty of enjoying these delicious children, now adults, reminiscing over a bottle of red wine and appreciating the planning their dad did to bring this trip together.

Justin has become a natural traveler. It is in his DNA now. Regardless of his physical health—okay, he did get sick while we were literally in line to check in for our flight one year—he is an enthusiastic travel companion. A pair of headphones, a good movie, and a hoodie to keep him comfortable, and he is good to go. His needs are few as well. Have you seen his suitcase? Perhaps one pair of pants and a couple of shirts is about all he needs. He has a thirst for different cultures and a yearning to immerse himself in the people and the music. The amazing thing about Justin also is that no matter where we are in the world, from Atlanta to Zagred (okay neither of us have been to Zagred, but you get the point), Justin can pick up his phone and message or Whatsapp someone and have a plan for the evening.

His passion for life stems from the experiences he shared

with each of his parents one on one. Amy took Justin on a trip to Thailand at the ripe age of eleven. The exposure to this unique country cemented his goal to travel the world. He has since lived in many places, including Jerusalem and Tel Aviv. When Justin was young, I spearheaded his first foray into music, a deep passion for which he has since cultivated and made uniquely his own. On our trips to basketball practice when he was a *very* young boy, my car would blast tunes ranging from The Who, *Live at Leeds*; Rage Against the Machine, *The Battle of Los Angeles*; or anything by Tupac. Is the statute of limitations up for DCFS to come after me? I know. Not the best lyrics to introduce then, but the emotion and the vibe was what mattered. We had a blast jamming to that music.

Justin's commitment to his mom at the end of her life and to me now fuel my pledge to parenting this amazing child/man/human without Amy, a job that will never have an expiration date.

Music, of course, had been one of the bedrocks of my marriage to Amy, as well as a big part of my life in high school and as a young man. I have seen some of the greatest bands in the world with my sister, Michel. Music always brought me to a specific moment in time, a memory, an experience that became a significant part of my life.

After Amy's death, listening to music took on new meaning. It brought me toward emotions that were the essential elements in the grieving process. I listened to plenty, and I cried a lot in my car alone. Luke Sital-Singh and Manchester Orchestra were crucial to helping me during some really dark times in those early months.

But listening to music and really engaging with it are two very different things, and the trip to Red Rocks helped me to understand that in a way I hadn't. In my grief, music had come to represent a coping mechanism, a way to help me with sadness. To my ears it lacked the joy, the release, that it had always possessed. After Red Rocks, all that changed. Music became something I pursued with a hunger and a passion that I hadn't possessed in years.

I sought out shows and regularly scanned venue schedules to see what new bands were being added, as I always had before Amy's diagnosis. The Chicago music scene quickly became a part of my routine again. While it was a helpful way to get me out the door, it was clear that this was about something more. As at Red Rocks, when I was out at a show I was able to uncover a part of myself that had been hiding, let loose just a bit, dance just a bit, laugh just a bit.

Experiencing music had been so important to my life with Amy, but rather than feel sadness when I was at shows without her, it felt like I was reconnecting with her, like perhaps I was starting to understand my blank space for the first time, to understand what she'd wanted for me, and what living my best life might actually look like.

Additionally, I made new memories for myself, and rediscovered the joy of seeing the kind of live music I really loved. Live music had always been something I felt deep passion for. Seeing a good band perform live made my soul feel deeply, made my body move to the beat, and allowed me to get lost and separate from the depths of grief, except when I trended toward those feelings, to deeply emote in a way only live music allows you to do.

After losing Amy, I went to shows by myself as well as with friends. Being alone allowed me to appreciate the music and the performance. I was also able to stand wherever I wanted to, unlike Amy, who was vertically challenged and always had to stand on the side of the stage to have any chance at a view.

I was also free to combine my passions for music and travel. If there was a good show in New York, I was all in. I went to Madison Square Garden for the first time ever to see Radiohead, and then Eric Clapton. I was in Brooklyn with my brother and best friend to watch the Class of 2017 be inducted into the Rock & Roll Hall of Fame. I hit all of the local venues in Chicago to see bands as varied as LP, Rhye, Bruce Hornsby, The Brian Jonestown Massacre, Amber Mark, LL Cool J, and many Manchester Orchestra shows. As you can see from the variety of artists, some were shows I could be found dancing at and others just jamming. Both of these feelings were emotional connections I could find only with live music. (I kept a list of all the shows I saw in one year.)

Obviously, it was a lot of music and a lot of travel, in between a whole lot of loss—either because of those losses or in spite of them, maybe some combination of both. There was excitement and joy in it. It made me feel alive. It saved me from spending too much time in my head, where it was too easy to get lost in all that darkness.

Besides, I had a blank page to fill.

15

Transitions

There's nothing like a blank page
You get to start from scratch
It could be anything, man, there's no catch
It's a good place for a dreamer
A good place for a dreamer to dream away
A blank page.

—Scott Mulvahill

I was making my way through my grief, albeit slowly. That blank space had some outlines on it, sketches of ideas. One thing I'd come to know for certain was that I didn't want to look back on this time in my life someday and find that I wasn't appreciating each day I had.

But of course, it's often just as you begin to feel your equilibrium returning that the ground shifts beneath you. Or at least that's how it happened for me.

Early in September 2017, after a summer spent reconnecting with the man I'd been, I decided to attend the wedding of some family friends with Miles. It seemed such an obvious choice at the time—I was saying yes to everything, why wouldn't I go?

The wedding was unique because it was one of the firsts for a friend whose child was getting married. It was also special because the mother of the groom had been one of Amy's close friends—mine as well, but they'd had a very special bond.

Still, though, what was I thinking?

There are so many triggers at weddings, as I learned from this experience. Seeing my friends walk in the beautiful sunlight to join their big family, their many friends, the wedding party, and these young, earnest, idealistic kids was wonderful. At the same time, I felt so deeply the permanent void in my own life. Amy would not be with me to see our children marry. We would never have that joyful moment of sending our kids off to their new life, to start their own family. Ugh, did that hit me hard in the gut. Such a juxtaposition between these two completely divergent emotions.

There was also the love emanating from the young couple getting married. They radiated everything that is good about thinking of the future of this planet—beautiful, smart, successful, emotional beings joining to make an impact. Would my own kids ever be so happy at their own weddings, I wondered, should they choose to marry? Or would this albatross hover over them always, prohibiting them from experiencing real joy for themselves? The emotional pain of thinking that way was very real.

I hadn't given much thought to the dancing part of the wedding festivities, either—obviously. I was getting used to doing many things on my own at this point—family dinners, out with friends, even live music. However, dancing with anyone at this wedding was not a proposition I had any interest in entertaining. In my previous life I'd loved to dance at weddings, at a party, at a concert—anywhere, really. Amy would always boost my confidence by telling me what a good dancer I was. She considered herself rhythmically challenged and did not think she was a good dancer at all, but we had so much fun dancing together. We would always be the last to leave the dance floor. But now the idea of dancing was unpleasant, to put it kindly. Yet another spark to remind me what I had lost.

And then there was table placement. It was hard enough that Amy was not there for me to talk to. Truth be told, even though Amy was much more extroverted than I, in a setting like this, we would have simply appreciated the time to sit together and visit, to talk and reflect. Now I was at the singles table. The first conversation I had turned out to be with a widow who looked me right in the eye and said, "I lost my husband seventeen years ago, and it doesn't get better." She went on to say she'd gone through phases of trying to date and had a miserable time. Thank you. That is just exactly appropriate to share with a new widower, very useful information—and so sensitive.

The culmination of all these factors prompted my early exit. Like I said, what was I thinking?

The aftermath of the wedding was tough. In many ways, it wasn't just the event that upset me, it was the fact that I hadn't seen my reaction coming at all; I'd been completely unprepared. Hard as I tried to put it behind me and press on, and to appreciate each day as it came, for a while it felt like all the progress I'd been making had been wiped out in a weekend.

Being emotionally overtaken by an unexpected, seemingly innocuous comment was something I became quite familiar with. When someone close to you dies, there's an assumption that the big events will be the hardest part—and they are indeed quite brutal. The first anniversary of Amy's death. The one-year anniversary of her memorial service. Her birthday, of course.

Family gatherings. Even events honoring Amy, well-intentioned and appreciated as they were, were harsh as hell.

But the thing about these big milestones is that at least you can see them coming and brace yourself, for all the good it does; the quieter moments—ambushes, as I've come to think of them—are a different story. I've had a much harder time with these surprises, which leap out at you with no warning when you're just going about your day and seem to reopen every deep wound you've been trying so hard to heal.

I'm religious about my annual checkup, and when I went to my first one after losing Amy, the receptionist slid a form in front of me, as always, and asked if all the information was still accurate. Instinctively I was going to answer yes when I looked more closely at the form.

"Emergency contact." No, that's not still accurate. Not at all.

"Marital status." Not that either. There's no box for "widower," by the way.

It was such a routine exercise, but it overwhelmed me with the sheer sadness of everything hiding beneath the surface, and the reality that I was alone now. I had a new life. A solitary life. There was even a moment of shock at the lack of tact, how thoughtless society can be when dealing with death.

Those days following that wedding were a dark time, one of the worst. Pick a random night from around then. Chances are, I was lying awake at some unreasonable hour. When people talk about the pain of grief, there's so much that can't be put into words, or even concrete feelings, just these flashes of emotion, powerful, gripping, blinding. Once they take hold, they are impossible to shake. Back when my insomnia used to keep me awake obsessing over little things before Amy got sick, in what felt like a previous life, it was often a snowball of anxiety. One thing I'd forgotten to do at the office became ten, building up momentum as I thought about all the other things I might have forgotten, until it was impossible to move my brain anywhere else. My sleeplessness in these days was different. Instead of having so many thoughts to juggle, I really had only two: missing Amy, and the vague fear that I wasn't living the life that she'd want for me. I felt a renewed connection to being an insomniac.

Of course I did emerge from it.

As I moved further away from Amy's death, that's largely how it went. Things would be improving, I'd be feeling better; then something would come along and yank me backward. And yet I never lost my momentum completely. Arrested as I felt at times, I could feel myself moving to a different place inside, shifting my vision forward to the future in a way that I hadn't been able to in months. That wedding with Miles had been a low point, perhaps the worst since Amy's death, but it was just that: a single point in my healing. There would be other low points, and I would deal with them as they came. But if I'd learned one thing from my meditation practice, it was that I couldn't spend time worrying about a future I couldn't prevent. I would take those moments one at a time; in the meantime, I focused on where I was—for good or bad.

This was largely my state of mind in late February 2018, as I was packing for a trip to San Francisco to attend a creative conference called Matter. They'd created a scholarship in Amy's name, and this would be the first annual award, presented to an artist whose work inspires a sense of community and connectedness.

By total coincidence, the award presentation was on March 3, 2018, the day after what would have been our twenty-seventh anniversary.

As I was packing for my trip to California, I found myself poking around in the closet Amy and I shared in the dream house we'd designed and built together. We'd intentionally placed the closet between our bedroom and the bathroom, so that we could share the beginnings and ends of our days together getting dressed and undressed. Not long after Amy's death though, I knew something had to change with that closet. Just walking through it had become impossibly hard. I have a family member who's left her husband's closet intact for years after his death. I didn't want that. I didn't need to be further reminded several times a day that Amy was gone.

The truth is, Amy never cared much for clothes. She would have been happy wearing a uniform every day—which she actually did, as a form of experimental art, for a while. But despite her relative lack of interest, after her death, her clothes had a way of catching my eye every time I walked past them, peripheral flashes of color accompanied by a requisite dose of painful reality. The cute long-sleeved shirt with the French lettering . . . and a sudden pang that we wouldn't be getting that flat in Paris we'd been talking about after all. That great little dress we bought for her in Thailand—what a beautiful trip that was, celebrating an anniversary, and now there would be no more of those.

In the days and weeks after Amy's death, it was still too soon for those memories to be happy ones. Thankfully, Amy's mom, siblings, sisters-in-law, and Paris came in and took out Amy's clothes for me. I stayed in the house but out of the way and put full trust in these wonderful women. I had set aside a few items

I wanted to keep for myself, memories I just couldn't part with. Mostly, I wanted my daughter to take whatever she wanted for herself and, who knows, maybe her kids someday.

When the clean-out was finished, only a few of Amy's items remained, hanging in the corner. Seeing the closet largely emptied of Amy's clothes was startling at first. At the same time, it felt just like my heart, a place where there would always be a small space that would go unfilled, permanently reserved for Amy.

I took the opportunity that the vacated space provided to move my own stuff around. In one of the empty spaces I reserved a couple of shelves for pictures of Amy and the kids and a few items of hers I was not sure what to do with. One of those piles on a shelf contained a few journals and books that I had never taken the time to fully investigate.

So there I was, packing for San Francisco, when I stumbled across a book on her side of the closet. As I looked at it closely, I saw the familiar handwriting on the cover, "for Jason," with her usual signature—a heart and "Amy" signed in her distinct cursive style, with the *y* attached to the *a* just so.

It hit me right in the gut.

Just looking at the cover, the curves of the letters leading to thoughts of what could be hiding inside, made me too sad to deal with it at that moment. Instead I decided to take it to San Francisco with me and read it on our anniversary a few days later.

On March 2, 2018, I quietly sat down in my hotel room and pulled the book out of my bag. I braced myself for it, but how do you brace for a tsunami?

Words is a whimsical, brilliant book by Christoph Niemann, illustrated with his own unique language of pictures. On each page is one simple word.

And on each page, Amy had written a message to me. It became more and more apparent as I read that this was a little project she'd undertaken and hidden away toward the end of her life.

One of the early pages in the book bore the word *paper*, for example, but Amy had added in her own handwriting, "I always said that I may be the writer in the family, but you truly know what to do with a piece of paper. Each of our children have been gifted a 'Jason letter' on many occasions."

On another page, with an image of a person with a sick face on both his face and his belly, Amy had written, "I think we should have been calling it 'collywobbles' all along!" The very next page, with the word *gobbledygook* and the image of a doctor conveying a diagnosis to a patient, included Amy's caption: "Yes, Amy, it looks like you have quite a bit of collywobbles and gobbledygook inside you."

I already had tears streaming down my face. Then I got to the entry that crushed me most. The image was of an ant carrying an apple several times its size. The word on the page was *carry*. The handwriting, shakier and clearly that of a sick person, read, "I will 'carry' you with me always and fo . . ."

Yes, this brilliant woman—who was *the* most particular person about grammar and typos and would call you on your shit if you sent her even a love note with an error in it—couldn't finish the sentence and left the page as is. Probably the result of a morphine-induced micronap. It broke my heart, and what would have been my twenty-seventh wedding anniversary ended up as a more intense day of grieving than I ever could have imagined.

One lesson I learned early on is that grief as a process is unique to everyone, and there is no right or wrong way to flow through it. This came much more clearly into focus as time went on and so many people shared their stories with me. By thrusting me into the spotlight, Amy had presented me with a path I never saw coming, but it was mine to take. Seeing this "word" book really hit me hard. I felt heartbroken that Amy had had to be so ill. The sudden wave of sadness was inevitable. I was resigned to the fact that my life would be an emotional roller coaster for the indefinite future, maybe always—one day I would be a wreck, the next, I'd stand tall as a representative of the Rosenthal family to honor Amy and help move her legacy permanently forward. I wasn't about to let her down, and I managed to smile my way through the Matter gathering and the awarding of the scholarship in her name.

It's a dichotomy that I realized would represent my life going forward, and indeed still does even now as I write these words. If I was going to speak about Amy, to honor her memory publicly, I needed to come to terms with the fact that my past, even the painful aspects of it, would be a part of my present and my future. It's not a decision everyone would make, but it's the one that felt right for me.

I am asked often whether carrying Amy with me always, and candidly telling everyone who will listen that it is an important part of my process, is like taking three steps forward and two steps back. In a word—no. I feel a healthy combination of accessing emotions about my loss that I do not mind returning to and a serene sense of my mission to keep Amy alive through talking about her and her uniquely gifted work. It is a message to the universe I think we need much more of as our planet gets more hostile and divergent. And personally, I feel good sharing her with the world, not only sharing my story but contributing my message of resilience as well.

Painful as it was, that conference, the book—the convergence of mourning and celebration of Amy on this day that had meant so much to us as a couple—all forced a realization upon me. In the year since Amy died, her life, her words, kept bringing me into contact with extraordinary new people. The essay in the *New York Times* had exposed a whole world of people to the woman that she was, and some of them now looked to me in ways that I never could have anticipated.

Her death had been covered in the nationwide press, from the *New York Times* to the *Chicago Tribune* to *People* magazine. Over five million people had read "You May Want to Marry My Husband" by the time she died; and since I was that husband, her spotlight inevitably spilled over onto me. I started hearing from a lot of women who'd lost their spouses, not with marriage proposals (yet) but with sweet, thoughtful, sincere condolences. In fact, two very accomplished women who'd been through public losses of their own reached out to share their experiences, openly describing the added intensity of grieving while strangers watch, and the helpless feeling of being at the mercy of unfamiliar emotions that are running wild. With time, they promised, joy would come if I let myself stay open to it. I couldn't imagine it.

Because of the national attention that Amy's death received, I also found myself descended upon by the media, and by— ready?—Hollywood producers. Shocking as it felt, I was "that husband," "that guy," so I guess there was an obvious logic to it, in someone's world. It wasn't my world, though, and I had no idea what to do. Wouldn't you know, it was another Amy who came to the rescue. Her name is Amy Rennert, and she was

Amy's literary agent and friend. They were as close as sisters, and she feels like a part of our family. She stepped right in on my behalf, setting up a protective force field around me and our family and handling this barrage of inquiries.

I'm sure my mouth was hanging open a little when Amy Rennert explained that some top Hollywood producers were interested in obtaining film rights to Amy's and my story and to some of her books. She encouraged me to at least listen to what these people had to say, sooner rather than later, so we could figure out who, if anyone, was the best fit. The idea of honoring Amy and perpetuating her exquisite messages by making a film about her life was definitely intriguing—Amy would have been ecstatic at the prospect.

Next thing I knew, we were on our way to Hollywood to "take meetings" with several very successful producers. Their bios were stellar, and their experience in the business was off the charts. For three days I collected myself emotionally and met one after another of these amazing people at a hotel in LA. Every single one of these superstars was warm, compassionate, and intensely interested in Amy and her legacy, and they came prepared. They'd dived deep into her vast body of work, from her published books to her films to her online presence to her résumé of public speaking engagements. I wasn't just impressed, I was very, very grateful.

Amy Rennert and I flew out of LAX to our respective homes wishing Amy had known these people. She would have been fast friends with many of them, and she would have had dozens of collaboration ideas, whether they involved a feature film or not. It was an incredibly stimulating trip, and both thrilling and intimidating to think of Amy, and our family, being portrayed on the big screen. Choosing the best team to make it happen and make it happen *right*, capturing the unique magic and contagious generosity of her spirit, was one of the most significant decisions I'd faced since Amy died. I was lucky to have Amy Rennert by my side—someone who knows us all, loved us as much as we loved her, and wasn't about to settle for anything but the best for us, and especially for Amy.

We ended up going with my first choice, a guy who shares a lot of my values, who reminds me of Paul, my father-in-law and role model, and who, as luck would have it, has Chicago connections.

The California trip was inspiring, and I came back more determined than ever not only to honor Amy's legacy but also put it to good, active use. Soon after I returned, I began the process of forming the Amy Krouse Rosenthal Foundation.

The mission reflects two causes important to Amy and our family: to support research in early detection of ovarian cancer, and to promote child literacy. I can't stress enough that I had no idea what I was doing. I had no qualifications to serve as the executive director and chairman of the board of a nonprofit organization. What I did have, though, was the full support of my entire family and the passionate involvement of a group of beautiful, supertalented people who agreed to serve on our initial board.

The Amy Krouse Rosenthal Foundation is small, and we're new, but we've already funded a researcher in Amy's name to see what kind of dent we can make in increasing awareness of the early signs of ovarian cancer, signs often ignored because they're so common among women: B is for persistent BLOATING that doesn't come and go; E is for difficulty EATING, and feeling full more quickly; A is for ABDOMINAL and pelvic pain felt on most days; and T is for TOILET, changes in urination or bowel habits. (And, guys, in case you haven't already figured this out, women are a lot tougher than we are, so they often battle through these symptoms without taking them seriously enough. Pay attention!) Early-stage ovarian cancer detection can result in a 90 percent survival rate, as compared to late-stage ovarian cancer, which has about a 20 percent survival rate and is unfortunately much more common.

As for child literacy, we have already donated tens of thousands of books to kids in need and are committed to many, many more being handed out over time. We have also engaged in programming geared toward kids to expose them to books at an early age, those formative years when we know reading is essential for a lifetime engagement with learning.

I can't begin to describe how proud I am of the Amy Krouse Rosenthal Foundation, and how fulfilled and grateful I am to be spending part of my time on this planet giving back, on Amy's and our family's behalf. And as usual, just when I thought Amy had enriched my life as much as she possibly could in the wake of her death, another door opened because of her, and all I had to do was say yes and walk on in.

All of this work on behalf of Amy's memory came to a crescendo in April 2018 when I walked on the main stage for a TED talk.

A member of the TED community approached me at the end of 2017 and invited me to give a talk at the upcoming main conference in Vancouver, Canada. In case you're not familiar with TED, it's a nonprofit global media organization that holds a main annual conference (and *many* others around the world).

Many of the talks are posted online in more than a hundred languages and cover a wide variety of subjects, with the slogan "Ideas worth spreading." TED stands for Technology, Entertainment and Design.

Amy had a relationship with TED. She'd spoken at TEDx conferences throughout the country (a TEDx event is a local gathering where live TED-like talks and performances are shared with the community) and assisted them with other creative projects, sometimes in collaboration with other artists, and she had enormous respect for the whole organization.

A million reactions flooded through my body, mind, and soul at the suggestion that I was even capable of doing something like this. I asked for some time to think about it.

What attracted me most to even the suggestion of telling my story publicly in this setting was the fact that I'd have control of the content. It was not an interview setting, where a talking head would drill me on my personal life, on the concept of Amy's essay being a personal ad, and on whether I'd found love yet. Here, I thought, I could control the message. If I agreed to write and deliver a TED talk, I could weave together my story the only way I knew how—being really honest about Amy and our relationship, the end of life, the treatment of the subject of death in our culture, loss of all types, the responses to Amy's article, and moving through and with grief to find some joy, happiness, and beauty. If they'd let me convey all that in my own way, why not give it a shot? I agreed to write a piece for TED.

Writing that TED talk was cathartic. It was also overwhelmingly emotional. I labored over every single word. When the script was as close to finished as I felt it was going to get, I submitted it to the powers that be, and they accepted it virtually as is.

I was on my way to giving a TED talk.

I spent the next couple of months far outside my comfort zone. I rehearsed that speech as if my life depended on it. Of course, I wanted to deliver—or, as a dear friend offered as a bit of coaching advice, "not suck." (Thanks again for that, Amy. Yes, yet another Amy R., AKR's college roommate and now my confidante on many subjects.) I wanted to nail it for Amy, for the thousands of people who'd reached out to me about Amy's essay, for my kids, for my family, and for the message itself. I practiced in front of the mirror. I practiced all over the house. I practiced in my law office. You name the place, I practiced there. I didn't share the content with my children or my family or my friends. I occasionally worked with a wonderful TED coach, but other than that, I was very private about what I was going to say.

I flew to Vancouver, walked nervously into the conference center, and promptly bumped into an old high school pal. He was surprised to see me. He was shocked when he saw this:

It turned out he was a TED veteran, and he couldn't have been more encouraging and supportive. Running into him after all those years at that time, at that place, felt like a sign that I'd made the right decision in agreeing to speak at this conference. My heart calmed from beating out of my chest to simply pounding as I headed to the greenroom to get ready. I was slated to give my talk on the Friday evening of the weeklong event, which ended Saturday morning. I could only imagine how many skilled, articulate, erudite acts I was following, and I wondered if I'd ever been this nervous in my life.

And then it was time. Paris was still in college in British Columbia, so as luck would have it, she was there, sitting in the audience to watch her dad succeed or fail at his first public-speaking gig. I went to the side of the stage to wait for my cue. Not until then, with two minutes to go, did I realize that I'd left my notes and my iPad in the greenroom. Oh, well. Too late now. I was about to stand naked, without a crutch, and deliver a speech in front of two thousand people.

I took a deep breath, stepped into that iconic TED red circle, and felt an immediate, surprising sense of calm as I dived in. Next thing I knew, I was saying, "Thank you." My fourteen min-utes were up, and my knees almost buckled with relief. I'd done it. I couldn't believe it. What a full, exhilarating feeling. I was inundated with positive, warm, emotional responses, but none meant more to me than the hugs and heartfelt praise I got from my daughter. She was moved. She was impressed.

As soon as the applause for the last talk of the evening faded away, the throngs descended on the basement of the conference center for the wrap party. There was plenty of food, drink, music, and dancing—and what do you know, I ran into another Chicago friend, this one a woman who was a fellow parent at my son's school for years. We started chatting, which evolved into dancing.

We were making our way around the dance floor when an-other dancing couple paused to acknowledge me and profusely thank me for the talk I'd given. We kept dancing. So did they. Step right, hips moving left. They introduced themselves. Shoulders swinging back in rhythm. They'd both been through significant losses as well. "My wife committed suicide a few months ago!" the man shouted over the music. Step right, now left. "Yeah, my husband died just a few months ago as well," the woman loudly announced. Shake a hip side to side.

It was a brief, remarkable scene—total strangers connecting on a dance floor over our devastating losses without missing a single step, sharing stories, understanding, caring, just being alive together with so few words, all set to music.

The balance between moving forward through grief and keeping my past life with Amy very much a part of what I have chosen to do with my blank page is a conflict I still think about and have been asked to comment on often. I can't imagine any other way, and honestly, I think Amy knew my path forward also. I touched upon this earlier, but it bears repeating: Amy had to have known that if her Modern Love column was published, it would be read widely. (I do not think she had any clue about the viral nature of what actually happened, but you get the point.) As a natural result of that, I would be the focus of attention in equal part to her gifted prose.

It has been so rewarding to keep Amy's legacy alive in my speaking and in my writing. Time has brought me joy—a lot of it—and an appreciation that I have so much to be grateful for. One of those gifts is my incredible life with Amy. Keeping her in my private life by grieving in my own way as well as talking about her publicly in my work has made me capable of processing how fortunate I was to have had what I did with her. I feel I am now at a place where I deeply appreciate that, though it has taken a while to get to that place, because grief is a complex and unforgiving beast. But how lucky was I, and how lucky are all of us who have been to the depths of intense grieving? We are the fortunate ones to have loved so deeply, or why else would we have such intense reactions to loss?

Almost immediately after my TED talk, I started fielding requests for speaking engagements. Apparently I was the new go-to guy on the subjects of loss and grief. I'll admit, it was a bit hard to know how to feel about this. Speaking about this regularly meant I'd be revisiting all of my challenges from the past year over and over again. I'd be moving forward by focusing on the past.

As time moves on, I move forward through and with grief, but also with a message of resilience added in. As that TED talk had revealed, I felt perfectly comfortable in that space.

16

Connecting

> When we die, our bodies become the grass, and the antelope eat the grass. And so, we are all connected in the great Circle of Life.
>
> —*Mufasa, in the* The Lion King

Some combination of Amy's *New York Times* essay, my TED talk, and public speaking inspired people from all over the world to write to me, wanting to connect about end-of-life issues, finding new meaning after loss, and ways to reclaim the joy, hope, and passion their loss seemed to have taken away.

There have been many, many letters, some of them in cursive longhand, and it deeply touches me that people in pain are moved to reach out to me, a total stranger, not just to tell their stories but to essentially say, "I'm sorry for your loss, and I understand, because I've been through it too." I've said it before, but it bears repeating—people are *good*.

As I began to get more requests for speaking engagements, I had to dig deep to make certain that I was committed to speaking about grief and loss while staying resilient at the same time. The power of the letters, emails, and packages I received made it clear that the work I was setting out to do was by far the most meaningful I had ever done. Having these incredible connections all over the world, even with total strangers, confirmed for me that I needed to keep talking openly about love, loss, and filling one's empty space.

These letters are also a clear reminder that loss is loss is loss. The death of a spouse, either suddenly or after a slow, painful illness. The death of a family pet. Losing a job after years of hard work. A medical condition that leads to a life-changing disability. Hitting rock bottom because of finances, or an addiction, or a mental disorder. Having to place a family member in memory care. Simply losing a dream. They all hurt. They all matter. And they connect us all when we reach out like Amy did, like these people did, and reassure us that, even if it's a stranger on the other side of the world, someone cares.

I could fill another entire book with the correspondence I received. I value each and every one of them. With the limited space I have here, I would like to share a few of these interactions with you to demonstrate the variety.

From a sixty-eight-year-old man who lost his wife of thirty-six years and his daughter within sixty days of each other:

> *I have tried to explain how a death of a spouse is so different. It is a creative process. When two people come together and build a life together over time, the whole becomes greater than the sum of the parts. Therefore, when a spouse dies, some part of the surviving spouse also necessarily dies. Part of me has certainly died.*

From someone wanting to share their home hospice experience:

> *Perhaps your talk resonated so strongly with me because so few people talk about the day-to-day horrors of seeing this beautiful human who you loved in everyday life decaying before*

*your eyes. I too carried my husband's 65 lb. body to the bath
and wrapped him up in cashmere so he could go outside just
once more in a wheelchair.*

From a newly single dad:

*The single dad thing has thrown me for a few loops and I am
definitely doing things I never expected (bra shopping for our
now 13-year-old daughter was interesting), but that we are still
here is what our wives wanted.*

There were messages that have inspired me to keep speaking
and, yes, even try my hand at writing a book . . .

*Thank you for your openness in . . . delivering your moving
TED talk (first and only time I've ever watched a TED talk).
While perhaps you didn't plan to be a public person, it is an
identity you wear with grace. Both you and Amy reached me
and touched me in ways few have.*

Divorcées reached out . . .

*"What will you do with your own fresh start?" This is the
question I am facing in the wake of unexpected divorce at the age
of 63. I alternate between horror and extreme excitement at the
possibilities.*

From a woman whose marriage ended:

> *I wish for you, Jason, a woman with an expansive ♥ who*
> *will always respect your love for Amy. I wish for your children*
> *that they'll allow themselves space and grace towards that*
> *woman—to like her when they like her, to dislike her if need be*
> *in those moments of their lives when they so desperately want*
> *their mom there, not her. There's complexity there for sure, but*
> *it can be done with respect for all.*

. . . and from people whose generosity reminded me so much of
Amy, and in some cases, moved me to tears . . .

> *The only thing I have been thinking since I was 18 years*
> *old is that if I could donate my life, my heart, my organs or*
> *whatever someone needs to survive. If I met your wife when*
> *she was diagnosed, I would definitely donate one of my ovaries*
> *as I wanted to donate my gallbladder to my mother.*

From a ten-page handwritten letter, accompanied by a dream
catcher:

> *I've faced so much sadness, abuse and many years of feeling*
> *hopeless and having so many questions about who I even was,*
> *since the years of abuse from a small child on to adulthood*
> *had brought on pretty severe PTSD. . . . I can only hope that in*
> *me sharing this with you, you'll be able to smile in your heart*
> *knowing Amy's beautiful presence on this earth is so strong that*
> *she touches people across the country without even knowing her.*

See, some people are good:

> *I am not sure exactly what I hope to achieve; maybe it's just a sounding board to capture my journey to share with you so you know you are not alone. And so I know I'm not alone.*

I've learned more from my wonderful new letter-writing friends from all over the globe than I can begin to describe. This woman, for example, whose mother died of ovarian cancer, introduced me in her letter to the Japanese tradition of *kintsukuroi*, the art of mending a broken pot with gold, making it even more precious than it was before. It was in that context that she concluded,

> *At the time Mom felt broken and the message comforted her. Today our lives have a brokenness, and future life will be very different, but hopefully with new beauty and encouraged by the legacy of love and kindness we've been given.*

In addition to these letters sharing extremely personal stories, I received all forms of religious missives, including a sincere note with a copy of the Book of Mormon, references to "doctors" all over the world who could eradicate Amy's cancer, as well as tchotchkes and symbols readers felt reminded them of Amy.

To every one of you who's taken the time and energy to share your stories, your pain, your thoughtfulness, your compassion, and your hope with me: whether or not we ever meet in person, we're connected now. Amy was a passionate believer in the power of connection. Through your generosity to me and our children, you've honored her legacy, and we thank you from the bottom of our hearts.

Hearing these stories made me think of *Free to Be . . . You and Me* and the lyrics "It's all right to cry / Crying gets the sad out of you / It's all right to cry / It might make you feel better." The memory of listening to *Free to Be* and reading these incredibly personal submissions made me want to shout to the rafters or post the following to a Facebook page. If I had one, I may have immediately posted the following thoughts that I think are so important for us guys to remember:

Grief and loss are a shared tale.

Somehow throughout the course of history, men have been labeled as unemotional. In fact, in institutions from the US military to our typical American family unit to our ball fields and sporting arenas, institutions of learning and their social groups, and even film and television, men are portrayed as rock-solid stoic types in the face of an emotional event. I have news for you: fuck that.

If you think you need permission, here it is. If your wife— the woman you built your family with, the lady you consider a model friend and mate, a vital cog in the wheel of universal creativity and the arts—dies, cry your eyes out. For that matter, if you lose your family pet, your job, your marriage, or your mate, let it out! For me, I bawled like a baby as my wife was rolled out of our home on a gurney. I cried my eyes out often afterward in my car when a familiar tune came on. I wept when one of my kids texted me. When I found my voice to relay my message about my experience with the end of life, I let it loose like a fountain as I practiced in the quiet of my home.

If you feel like you need to talk about your pain, do so. Just because my journey through loss and my grief was more public than the average person's does not make me the only guy to want to share how it feels at the end of the life of someone you love, or to suffer loss of any kind, for that matter. I am here to say, "It's okay to talk about how you feel." Find a way that works for you, whether that is with one good friend, a family member, or the neutrality of a mental health professional. Again, this is just me, but talking with a therapist was vital for my process.

If you need to find a place to talk anonymously, share your story with me at jasonbrosenthal.com.

Just please let us shout it to the rooftops: guys, it is really acceptable to show emotion when you go through a loss of any kind. Period.

Of course, because Amy's New York Times essay was called "You May Want to Marry My Husband," there's a whole other category of mail that still keeps coming. You guessed it—many, many women have reached out to me to extoll their virtues as my potential new spouse. Some are very genuine, carefully and thoughtfully handwritten. Some are hard to understand but convey a genuine sentiment. And some have just made me laugh. I can't always tell if that was the intention, but it doesn't keep me from appreciating the result.

Amy must have known that there would be a response when her essay was published. That the response has been so overwhelming, and from all corners of the globe, probably wouldn't have surprised her one bit, but it still surprises me. There were crates full, but here are a couple of examples:

To Amy, a day or two after her essay went viral:

I, like so many others, just read your moving article/profile
about your husband, Jason, and I want to introduce myself.
You see, I am his future wife, or rather, someone like her.

This one made me smile, too, and scratch my head a little.

I mean, I do love a good tequila, but . . . really?

I'd been receiving these notes ever since Amy's piece was published, and as I put myself out there more with the TED talk, they just kept coming. I always approached them with humor and a well of gratitude for the sentiments they expressed.

On Father's Day, 2018, an essay I wrote in response to Amy's was printed in the *New York Times* Modern Love column—essentially my love letter back to her:

My Wife Said You May Want to Marry Me

Illustration by Brian Rea.

I am that guy.

A little over a year ago, my wife, Amy Krouse Rosenthal, published a Modern Love essay called "You May Want to Marry My Husband." At 51, Amy was dying from ovarian cancer. She wrote her essay in the form of a personal ad. It was more like a love letter to me.

Those words would be the final ones Amy published. She died 10 days later.

Amy couldn't have known that her essay would afford me an opportunity to fill this same column with words of my own for Father's Day, telling you what has happened since. I don't pretend to have Amy's extraordinary gift with words and wordplay, but here goes.

During our life together, Amy was a prolific writer, publishing children's books, memoirs and articles. Knowing she had only a short time to live, she wanted to finish one last project. We were engaged then in home hospice, a seemingly beautiful way to deal with the end of life, where you care for your loved one in familiar surroundings, away from the hospital with its beeping machines and frequent disruptions.

I was posted up at the dining room table overlooking our living room, where Amy had established her workstation. From her spot on the couch, she worked away between micro-naps.

These brief moments of peace were induced by the morphine needed to control her symptoms. A tumor had created a complete bowel obstruction, making it impossible for her to eat solid food. She would flutter away on the keyboard, doze for a bit, then awake and repeat.

When Amy finished her essay, she gave it to me to read, as she had done with all of her writing. But this time was different. In her memoirs she had written about the children and me, but not like this. How was she able to combine such feelings of unbearable sadness, ironic humor and total honesty?

When the essay was published, Amy was too sick to appreciate it. As the international reaction became overwhelming, I was torn up thinking how she was missing the profound impact her words were having. The reach of Amy's article—and of her greater body of work—was so much deeper and richer than I knew.

Letters poured in from around the world. They included notes of admiration, medical advice, commiseration and offers from women to meet me. I was too consumed with grief during Amy's final days to engage with the responses. It was strange having any attention directed at me right then, but the outpouring did make me appreciate the significance of her work.

When people ask me to describe myself, I always start with "dad," yet I spent a great deal of my adult life being known as "Amy's husband." People knew of Amy and her writing, while I lived in relative anonymity. I had no social media presence and my profession, a lawyer, did not cast me into public view.

After Amy died, I faced countless decisions in my new role as a single father. As in any marriage or union of two people with children, we had a natural division of labor. Not anymore. People often assumed Amy was disorganized because she had list upon list: scattered Post-it notes, scraps of paper and even messages scrawled on her hand. But she was one of the most organized people I have ever met.

There are aspects of everyday life I have taken on that I never gave much consideration to in the past. How did Amy hold everything together so seamlessly? I am capable of doing many things on my own, but two people can accomplish so much more together and also support each other through life's ups and downs.

Many women took Amy up on her offer, sending me a range of messages—overly forward, funny, wise, moving, sincere. In a six-page handwritten letter, one woman marketed her automotive knowledge, apparently in an effort to woo me: "I do know how to check the radiator in the vehicle to see if it may need a tad of water before the engine blows up."

While I do not know much about reality TV, there was also this touching letter submitted by the child of a single mother, who wrote: "I'd like to submit an application for my mom, like friends and family can do for participants on 'The Bachelor.'"

And I appreciated the sentiment and style of the woman who wrote this: "I have this image of queues of hopeful women at the Green Mill Jazz Club on Thursday nights. Single mothers, elegant divorcées, spinster aunts, bored housewives, daughters, wilting violets . . . all in anxious anticipation as to whether the shoe will fit, fit them alone, that the prince from the fairy tale is meant for them. That they are the right person."

I could not digest any of these messages at the time, but I have since found solace and even laughter in many of them.

One thing I have come to understand, though, is what a gift Amy gave me by emphasizing that I had a long life to fill with joy, happiness and love. Her edict to fill my own empty space with a new story has given me permission to make the most out of my remaining time on this planet.

If I can convey a message I have learned from this bestowal, it would be this: Talk with your mate, your children and other loved ones about what you want for them when you are gone. By doing this, you give them liberty to live a full life and eventually find meaning again. There will be so much pain, and they will think of you daily. But they will carry on and make a new future, knowing you gave them permission and even encouragement to do so.

I want more time with Amy. I want more time picnicking and listening to music at Millennium Park. I want more Shabbat dinners with the five of us Rosies (as we Rosenthals are referred to by our family).

I would even gladly put up with Amy taking as much time as she wants to say goodbye to everyone at our family gatherings, as she always used to do, even after we had been there for hours, had a long drive home ahead of us and likely would see them again in a few days.

I wish I had more of all of those things, just as Amy had wished for more. But more wasn't going to happen for her or us. Instead, as she described, we followed Plan "Be," which was about being present in our lives because time was running short. So we did our best to live in the moment until we had no more moments left.

The cruelest irony of my life is that it took me losing my best friend, my wife of 26 years and the mother of my three children, to truly appreciate each and every day. I know that sounds like a cliché, and it is, but it's true.

Amy continues to open doors for me, to affect my choices, to send me off into the world to make the most of it. Recently, I gave a TED Talk on the end of life and my grieving process that I hope will help others—not something I ever pictured myself doing, but I'm grateful for the chance to connect with people in a similar position. And of course I am writing to you now only because of her.

I am now aware, in a way I wish I never had to learn, that loss is loss is loss, whether it's a divorce, losing a job, having a beloved pet die or enduring the death of a family member. In that respect, I am no different. But my wife gave me a gift at the end of her column when she left me that empty space, one I would like to offer you. A blank space to fill. The freedom and permission to write your own story.

Here is your empty space. What will you do with your own fresh start?

Humbly, Jason

17

Burning

The journey has been hard, but some really exciting experiences have blossomed because I was willing to dip my toe into new waters.

—*Howard Stern*

It's very common to describe the grief process as a journey, and yes, it's most definitely that—a rough one, with no straight lines, and you find yourself believing you're always going to feel like this. It's very different for everyone who goes through it, and very much the same. Perhaps that's why in hindsight it's so surprising that part of my journey led me to Burning Man.

I suppose it makes a certain amount of sense. After all, Burning Man had been on Amy's and my Empty Nest list from what seemed like a lifetime ago. Both Amy and I had been very curious about Burning Man, based on a vague notion of what it was all about. Why not give that a try?

Burning Man is an annual late-summer event held at Black Rock City, a temporary community built in the Black Rock Desert in Nevada. It started as a small beach party in San Francisco in 1986. It's grown into a nine-day gathering of around eighty thousand people from all walks of life, there to engage in communal experiences of art, transformative change, participation, overcoming the barriers that stand between us and our inner selves and those around us, and, in the end, head back to their lives leaving no physical trace behind, out of respect for the environment.

I talked about Burning Man with an old high school buddy I'd reconnected with at a reunion, and later at the TED conference. He had been the previous year, and we agreed that I'd meet him and his girlfriend in their RV in Black Rock City. I had no real idea what to expect; I just followed instructions from the intense suggested packing list for the potentially severe extremes of the Nevada desert between the scheduled dates of August 26 to September 3, 2018. I made one and only one promise to myself: No expectations, just go with the pace of what the experience has to offer and take full advantage of the Burning Man grieving temple.

The public perception of Burning Man seems to be that it's a huge, hedonistic nine-day party. I'm here to tell you that it was much, much more than that for me. It opened my eyes, my mind, and my heart to a whole new kind of adventure I wasn't sure I'd have the courage to survive. It was hot, dirty, dusty, cold, dirty, uncomfortable, dirty, and loud. It was also beautiful, deep, moving, intense, loving, open, welcoming, and new. I attended talks about relationships and new political parties and tapping (a combination of acupressure and psychology in which you tap your fingertips on meridian points of the body while talking about upsetting memories and other emotional issues) as well as a lecture about ayahuasca (a centuries-old herbal drink used in religious and healing ceremonies). I danced in the cold at sunrise. I grooved to the art cars blaring DJ sets at night. I drank a Bloody Mary at two in the afternoon.

I was also exposed to a new language at Burning Man. I began to notice that people were using words that they all knew, but

I had no idea what they were saying. My friend quickly noticed my bewilderment at these new terms. I began to write these new expressions in my journal. As Rob picked up on this process, every time a new concept was introduced, we would crack up as though we were back in high school doing something inappropriate behind a teacher's back. (Actually, Rob would never have done that back then, but I definitely was inclined to drift in that direction.) Here are some of the new words and concepts: drop in, juicy, the field, co-creation, weaving the web, divine masculine/feminine, resonance, sacred container, feeling known, integrating, and state change. What had I gotten into?

And I found the most incredible community grieving spot I've ever seen or read about. The Burning Man grieving temple is devoted to acknowledging, reflecting on, and learning from grief. The walls bear offerings to the deceased. These ranged in complexity from the mere scrawling of a name on the walls of

The community grieving spot at Burning Man.

the temple to complex art pieces constructed in their memory. I brought my own versions for Amy, my dad, and, most freshly at the time for me, our dog Cougar.

It had been less than a month since Cougar died, on July 26, 2018, a year to the day after my dad died. I was at my downtown office when our dog walker called to say that something was going on with Cougar—he'd lain down after their walk and refused to get back up again. She was right, that sounded nothing like him, and Cougar and I were at the veterinarian's office within the hour.

Another thirty minutes later the vet gave me the news. It seems Cougar had suffered spontaneous internal bleeding. I had two choices: Put our cherished fourteen-year-old dog through a major, life-threatening surgical procedure with no guarantee of success, or let him go.

It's a decision every pet owner dreads, and I knew I couldn't make it by myself. I needed Amy—she would have known what to do. I didn't have her to turn to, but I had Miles. He should be here. He had to be here, if only to say goodbye. Cougar had joined our family when Miles was only nine years old. It was Miles who took the reins and trained that big spunky puppy when he first arrived; and while we all adored that dog, no one loved him more than Miles did. It didn't take long for the two of us to agree that, excruciating as it was, we loved Cougar enough to spare him major surgery and a long, impossible-to-predict recovery and just let him quietly, painlessly go to sleep.

The vet couldn't have been more sensitive and sympathetic. She asked if we wanted to be in the room while Cougar was euthanized. I couldn't do it. I couldn't watch another family member essentially die in my arms. Miles heroically stepped up, and was there with Cougar when he took his last breath.

Amy is stuck in my brain at age fifty-two. Relatively speaking, that's a youthful, beautiful age; but I have a lasting different image of Amy from the final two months of her life. I wish that freeze-frame was a healthier one. Cougar, on the other hand, will always be a playful, happy black Lab mix, even with the gray goatee he'd been sporting for the past couple of years.

If you've never loved and been loved by a pet, it's hard to describe how devastating it is to lose one. If you have, you don't need me to tell you. Whoever coined the saying "I hope to become the person my dog thinks I am" knew exactly what they were talking about. For fourteen years, no matter what the rest of the world seemed to think of me, every time I walked in the door, whether I'd been gone for two weeks or two minutes, Cougar greeted me with an insanely wagging tail and a busily sniffing nose as if seeing me was the most joyful thing that had ever happened to him. And all he asked for in return was some kibble, a good scratch behind the ears or on his belly, and a nice walk. He was treasured by each and every member of our family. He was there as the kids and cousins grew up, right there to protect them as they learned how to swim and play in the pool—there he'd be, pacing up and down at the edge of the pool, agitated, thinking they might be in danger, and he wouldn't relax until they were safely out of the water again.

The chain of losses, from Amy to Arnie to Cougar, felt like being kicked in the gut time and time again as I was trying so hard to regain my footing. I felt powerless against the overwhelming message that, ready or not, you'd better always be prepared to say goodbye. I guess that's why it wasn't surprising I went to the grieving temple every day of the festival. I needed to.

I sat in silence and wept, side by side with other mourners, each of us deep in the throes of our solitary grief but profoundly connected without saying a word. Hugs were shared. Tears flowed. It was a huge milestone in my healing journey, and more than worth the dirt, dust, heat, cold, noise, and crowds that were the cost of attending.

For some reason, I would remember a random thought about Amy while I was in the desert. One that came to mind was early in our relationship. We were well into our button business, scouring flea markets for interesting buttons and spending a good deal of our free time making sure we had enough product. When we had ample inventory, we registered for space to sell our wares at an outdoor artist's market that was popular in Chicago at the time. The event was called Market Days and was held near our home, in an area affectionately known as Boystown, one of the largest LGBT communities in the midwestern United States. Amped with the enthusiasm that she brought to most things in life, Amy invited her parents down to visit us at our booth.

Now, Ann and Paul are two of the most amazing parents anyone can imagine. They showered Amy with love from day one of her existence and taught her so many of the values she carried with her into her migration to adulthood: love and kindness, hard work, family, and a message to give back to those not as fortunate as her family was. However, they were definitely, by their own admission, more 1950 than 1990 at the time of this art show. They supported Amy always, cheering her on from the sidelines without hesitation, and they agreed to come down and visit us there and see what the art fair was like. Little did any of us know that the crowd was, how shall I say, not 1950! There were boys in bikinis and girls on skateboards. Men with nipple piercings and sweaty bodies.

Amy's parents were incredulous. They could not believe that we thought they would want to be a part of that scene. It became a story told time and again throughout our entire marriage. Sitting there in the temple, the story made me smile, thinking about Amy and her infectious lust for life.

The trip to Burning Man happened only a year and five months after I'd lost Amy. But a year and five months on the journey through loss and grief is a good distance. My path already felt like a roller coaster—I had moments of joy and other times of profound sadness. Attending this truly unique experience, however, was unlike any other part of my odyssey thus far.

Because my entire being was so open to any experience at Burning Man, my heart was open as well. As I sat in the grieving temple, I could close my eyes and weep deeply. And I could sit with those feelings for as long as I needed to. My tears flowed for my Amy and for what we had together and for what we were missing out on. Soon, when I was ready to, I left the others grieving and biked back to my RV. Within hours, I was dancing to the "oontz, oontz" of the DJ music emanating from multiple locations. This process made it clearer to me that my life might just be this way, and that it was okay. One moment I might be really deep in my grief, and the next I might find myself discovering joy in my new life.

By the end of the festival, I was exhausted yet oddly energized. I'd done something Amy and I had talked about doing together, so there was a certain feeling of mission accomplished, especially since she would have loved it there. I was pretty much on my own, left to step out of my introverted comfort zone and find my way in the foreign space of Black Rock City, and I did it.

Burning Man isn't necessarily for everyone. But I think it forced me to confront things that were still lingering beneath the surface, things that I still had to purge, and I needed the space and lack of judgment to do it. Not everyone needs this, nor should they. For me, though, this experience was difficult to quantify but absolutely crucial to my healing process.

There are quite a few takeaways from my Burning Man experience, and many reasons my first trip there wasn't my last. My sense of accomplishment, having navigated this process as a solo mission, helped me accept that I could continue to fill my blank page with fascinating experiences on my own. I learned that I was thirsty for and willing to fill my life with new, unfamiliar exploration. Even though I might be anxious about attending a conference, traveling on my own, or meeting new people, this trip allowed me to feel the power of being enlightened by the unfamiliar.

Something happens at Burning Man that is transformative for me, not just for the time I am physically there but for a long time afterward as well. It is like no other place in the "default world," as everyday life is called by Burners. Certainly, the setting contributes to that feeling. In the middle of nowhere. No cell service. No showers. No plumbing at all . . . you get the point. That, combined with the fact that I felt perfectly comfortable sporting gold pants and a black fur coat while riding my bike in the cool evenings, made it clear that my mind and body were free to express themselves and absorb feelings in a totally different way.

18

Deepening the Loss

I Get this Feeling of Impending Doom...
Is there Something You're Not Telling Me?

—*Tom Wilson, writing as Ziggy as he stares up to the sky*

I was entrenched in my solo life and experiencing new things in the fall of 2018. I felt happy at times, a bit wabi-sabi at others, but the darkest moments were fading somewhat. I had even planned a wonderful trip for the kids and me during the winter holiday. And that's when I was thrown once again.

We got the news that the small spot of cancer on my father-in-law Paul's lung had traveled through his bloodstream to form a mass in his brain. Brain surgery was essential.

Paul had been devastated by the loss of his eldest daughter. He was fond of saying that he went to a grief counselor once who told him that "everyone grieves differently." I think that gave him permission to feel okay about not crying, even though he and Ann talked about the impact it had on the two of them when they were in private conversation.

After I delivered my TED talk, he was effusive about how well I had done. Because of my deep respect for him, this filled me with confidence about my path forward. He was fond of telling anyone who would listen that after watching me deliver the talk, he thought I should tell the producers of Amy's film that I should play myself. Paul was never shy about making his opinions known, but he always did it in an endearing way. The sudden possibility of losing him was crushing.

Our family, our pack, did what we do—we descended on the hospital en masse to ride out the wait together. Brain surgery isn't a quick procedure, so we whiled away the day reading, working, pacing, eating, and reflecting, staying positive every minute. I wore a sticker I found in Amy's drawer that read, "Feeling pretty good about this."

Sure enough, Paul made it out of surgery. Sadly, though, he never bounced back to his old happy, smiling, hot-dog-eating, shirt-stained-from-food-inhaling, corny-joking, exercise-hating, Cubs-loving, Ann-adoring, family-heading self. And sadly, before long we found ourselves in the awful, familiar setting of home hospice again. Three generations gathering for Paul and for one another, not just needing to be there but *wanting* to be there, because it was him, because we wouldn't have dreamed of being anywhere else.

Ann and I shared long, open, honest conversations about end-of-life issues and wished we weren't getting so good at them. "Talk about it," I told people at speaking engagements. Confront the reality that death will surely come. Exactly when, who knows?

I was much less fearful of the home hospice experience we were going through with Paul because of what Amy and I and our family had to endure. In a way, I was hyperaware of the beauty in the room when Paul, the patriarch, was surrounded by his family and his devoted spouse. I was able to talk to him even when it was unclear what he processed. I was able to touch him lovingly, even when there was no physical response. I was able to observe the sheer beauty of seeing this loyal pack experiencing yet another devastation together.

Then I'd go home at night, climb into bed, and try to fall asleep while wondering if I'd ever see Paul again. I distinctly remember springing up one morning at 3:00 a.m., knowing exactly what I would say to him and feeling compelled to write it in my journal:

Can I talk to you about something?
I know you have not been feeling good/yourself and I am so sorry.
I want you to know that I understand if it is too uncomfortable, too overwhelming.
If it is too much, I get it.
I want you to know a couple of things:
You are a role model to me;
The way you are as a husband, as a businessman, as a father to me and especially to Amy and a grandfather to our children is so incredible and inspiring;
Thank you for making me so much a part of the Krouse family.

*If you are too overwhelmed and too tired and you sometime
leave this physical world, please give Amy a big hug and kiss—
tell her I love her every day* so *much.*

I quietly read it to him in a private moment. He only nod-
ded, but I knew he got it.

I would not have known how to convey such specific feelings
before I discovered how to do it myself after Amy's death. That
is part of why I take on that mission in my life now. But Paul
and I shared many, many private moments in my twenty-eight
or so years of knowing this spectacular man.

I remember clearly sitting outside at the Krouses' Florida
home when the kids were quite young. At the time, Paul had a
propensity to enjoy a cigar on occasion. It took a special moment to break one out together. The moment I am thinking
about, Paul broke out a stogie and we simultaneously enjoyed
a nice scotch. It was a quiet moment I never had with my own
father. Our conversation covered topics from raising kids, to
the importance of family, to what it would take for the Cubs to
compete. It was one of many moments I will never forget about
Paul.

We were all together, surrounding our patriarch, when his
final moments came. The scene was stunningly beautiful, if you
can call such finality beautiful. Truly, though, the fact that the
last thing this sensational human being, this leader of his family, saw in this lifetime were the many faces of those who absolutely treasured him seemed like the way we should all aspire to
leave this world someday.

I'd managed to be stoic and present for my kids throughout
Paul's time in hospice. When he was officially gone, my sense of

serenity cracked, my pent-up sorrow boiled over, and it was my kids who were comforting me through my uncontrollable sobs, a tidal wave of grief catching up to me.

At the time of Paul's passing, I had endured the loss of my wife, my dad, and our sweet family pet Cougar. Paul absolutely adored his firstborn, and he was crazy about Cougar. (I can hear him say "Cougs" or "Cougie" even now.) Each new loss was like a body blow from Mike Tyson, physically and emotionally. Compounding my own experiences with loss, at this point I had been talking a great deal about navigating through grief and loss to throngs of others in public forums.

In a profound way, my own experiences of loss made me a better messenger to discuss this issue. Having these personal experiences absolutely made me a better listener. I connected with and appreciated in a deeper way so many around the world who shared their stories with me—not just about death, but about all of the types of loss people experience in this world that I have written about thus far in these pages. In addition, I became a better student about all aspects of the grieving process. Reading what others experience, observing the ways people deal with grief, and being inspired by how resilient people can be permitted me to move forward both personally and in my new path as a public speaker.

All of which, I'm sure, contributed to the fact that, a few days after Paul's death, I somehow managed to get through delivering my third eulogy in less than two years:

There are two essential life lessons I learned from Paul Krouse. The first is a commitment to fitness and taking care of your body. And, of course, the second is a lifelong dedication to healthy eating choices. [*Pause for laughter.*]

While it is fun to joke about Paul—he was a very funny man—the truth is that he was, far and away, my biggest role model in life.

…

As you all know, our family has had their fair share of loss over the last few years. I have delved extensively into the subject of death and dying. I can promise you that the end of Paul's life was extraordinarily beautiful, and his grandkids will always remember that death is a part of life.

Now, I am also here as a representative of Paul's oldest daughter Amy. Amy LOVED her daddy. At the point in Amy's life when she started to become known as an accomplished author, Paul would always remind people (anyone who would listen, really) that before any fame—and way more important than her literary and speaking accomplishments—Amy was a genuinely good person. I know that even with all of Paul's own success, we can agree that the same is true about him.

I would like to conclude with some of Amy's own words. These are from her memoir, so the "she" Amy writes about is her:

> 1970—Practices swimming in pool with father. She starts on stairs, he stands waiting a few feet away. Just as she approaches him, he takes a step back. He keeps doing this. He is encouraging about it, but she is nervous, out of breath. Doesn't want to keep going… just wants to be swept up in his arms when she reaches him. The relief, the *snugness*, the glory of finally being in Dad's safe arms.

If you believe in such things, I hope you envision Amy's number-one cheerleader joining her now for a magnificent safe embrace.

Paul's loss was hard. In many ways it was harder than the loss of my own father.

By December 2018, my journey through loss and grief had taken many twists and turns. I was asked, for example, to return to the Matter gathering, this one in Los Angeles. However, this time I was one of the presenters, delivering a talk on love, grief, loss, and resilience. My mother was in the audience. At that point, a large component of my message was to talk candidly about end-of-life issues, home hospice, and how we humans deal with such intense loss yet carry on with our lives.

Once again, I had to face all those questions from a personal perspective. Certainly, I was much more self-aware of the effects deep loss had on me and my family. I was also quite familiar with the hospice experience. I answered the very questions I pose to audiences: "How much can the human condition handle? What makes us capable of dealing with these intense losses and yet carry on?" The answer: It is a lifelong mission. I, however, had Amy's express permission to absorb the most intense loss imaginable and be told clearly that I had to go on with making a new life. I feel obligated to share that mission with the universe, both here and in my speaking life. It is so, so hard. I wish none of these losses formed my own story, but they do. My personal experiences have allowed me to appreciate what I have and permit me to share what I have learned with you.

19

Have You Remarried Yet?

I wanna show you, how I've grown in this place
In this place, I'm not alone and I know I'll be okay

—*Luke Sital-Singh*

It's a hard thing for me to talk about, let alone write about, but I promised myself that I'd be as open and honest about everything as my inherently private nature allows. I tell people to talk about loss and about end-of-life issues, yes . . . In other words, this is a topic I have never talked about, but I feel it is important to lend permission to others in my position. Not talking about dating feels dishonest.

I've talked to a lot of widows and widowers since Amy died, and there's no doubt about it, we each have our own timetable and our own unique path toward healing and moving on. There's no rulebook, no right or wrong, no should or shouldn't, no too soon or not soon enough. I have a family friend who lost his wife more than six years ago and still shudders at the thought of dating. I've met men and women who were married within months of losing a spouse, and others who have no intention of it.

I slowly became aware that I was missing the companionship of a woman, which I hadn't had in a good couple of years. My sole purpose, my life's mission for the two years before Amy died, had been taking care of Amy and getting her healthy again. That turned into being her caretaker, which was intense and laser-focused and all that mattered to me. I couldn't deny that now there was something appealing about the idea of sharing a meal, a good cocktail, and some music with a woman who'd enjoy them as much as I do.

Amy hadn't just given me her blessing to find love again, she'd actually encouraged it. I talked to each of my kids separately to ask how they felt about my dating in general, and they gave me nothing but sensitive, understanding support, as did the rest of my family and my close confidantes.

And to be clear, once I'd determined I was open to dating, it didn't mean that I started actively looking, that's for sure. I had no interest in Tinder, or Bumble, or eHarmony, or any of those other online dating sites, just as Amy mentioned in her viral essay. I still don't. I knew that if I was going to start to date again after thirty years of being out of the game, it was going to have to happen organically or not at all.

The first "encounter," if you can call it that, happened at an exercise class. One of the women there was particularly attractive. After class we spent a few minutes chatting about the intensity of the workout and other small talk, and I left wondering, had I just been flirting with that woman? Logically, I knew that even if I was, it was harmless and perfectly okay. But honestly, emotionally, it felt like I was cheating on Amy. The visceral conflict was palpable.

Not long after that, a buddy and I had tickets to a concert by a band Amy and I loved. He canceled at the last minute, but there was no way I was going to miss that concert. I went by myself and found myself in a similar situation—smart, sexy younger woman, casual conversation, very sultry on the dance floor. I tried to just relax and have a good time.

I consider Amy's express permission in her piece to begin another love story a real gift. As I started to think about dating, I was not thinking about love. It was enough to walk around the streets of my own city, my community, with someone other than Amy. I felt guilty and kept looking over my shoulder. When I was asked about what Amy's message meant to me, I told the world that her blessing has been a guide for me in the most meaningful way. It permitted me to even think about other women, dating, and the idea of a relationship with someone else.

Having said that, everything was and remains complex. It's no secret that Amy occupies a place in my heart and always will. Knowing that makes whoever wants to be with me a unique and openhearted individual, and any relationship I might find myself in would have to be predicated on the notion that my past is still going to be a part of my present and my future.

It was some time later that I happened to meet a hazel-eyed identical twin. Again, I wasn't looking for her, but after we'd spent some time together, I knew there was something special about this woman, and my world changed.

We started seeing each other, and the companionship, *her* companionship, felt so good. Even then, when she and I started going out in public, I was still apprehensive about being judged for enjoying myself with a woman who wasn't Amy.

My kids, my family, my best friend, and my therapist talked me through it, and I finally got it that all the disapproval and judgment I was so braced for was self-imposed. Everyone who loved me, especially Amy, just wanted me to be happy. I was the one who'd been holding out, afraid that if I let myself be happy without Amy, I'd be dishonoring her, betraying her somehow.

What I finally came to realize was that being happy again would actually be, in a way, a testament to the thirty beautiful years I'd had with Amy, and my memories of them that, no matter what happens along the way, I'll cherish for the rest of my life. It's because of her that I know I have the capacity to love deeply and to embrace every minute of joy I can possibly create.

Amy left that blank page at the end of her essay for me to compose my fresh start. I get it that it would be perfect to end this story by explaining that the empty space has been filled. I am certainly open to that. I think the larger point is that there is that intentional empty space. I ask myself often, as I ask many people I have been exposed to over the last several years, what I will do with my blank page, with my fresh start. In many ways, I answer that question every day. With new experiences. With an entirely new perspective on seeing the world. With a woman I think about many times throughout the day. With mindfulness and an open heart.

Thank you, Amy, for giving me that gift.

A Permanent Place to Gather

Please, sir, may I have some more?

—*Charles Dickens*

Not long ago a close family member asked me, "When are you moving? Aren't there ghosts everywhere?" A little crass, I guess, but I understood the desire to protect me from too many memories and too much loneliness.

Whether to pack up and leave or stay right where you are is an intensely personal decision after you've lost a spouse you treasured, a decision no one can really make but you. I completely get it that staying is unbearable for some people. For me, at least for now, it would be unbearable for me to leave my house, to go home to some new place after a day's work or an evening out or a weekend with the family or a trip.

I've mentioned several times that this was Amy's and my dream house, and there's no other way to describe it. We built it together from the ground up, on the same site as the little frame house we bought together, on a tree-lined residential street that's about a ten-minute walk from Wrigley Field. When our kids came along and we realized we were running out of space, we hired my best friend Jeff as our general contractor, tore down the frame house, and started over. What we created can best be described as a modern farmhouse, with fabricated wood paneling on the outside and a whole wall of bookshelves on the inside that extends from the basement to the third floor, because we could, because we wanted to, because that was so much of who Jason&Amy were.

We made every single decision about every single detail as a team, but the house has Amy's imprint, her unique artistic sensibility and her quirky style, everywhere you look.

We raised our family here together. We created here together, and cooked here together, and had Shabbat dinners and Backwards Nights here. We made life plans together here. Cougar spent fourteen years here with us. Amy wrote here, and I developed my own sense of art and style here. The playfulness of the powder room on the first floor was my pet project—sparkly wallpaper, and a magnificent clear chandelier with red accents. My own idiosyncratic habits evolved here. Adjusting the shades in the living room just so, organizing the firewood so that it was stacked exactly right, placing the three digitally printed pieces of art representing our children's images in a neat row on our chest of drawers. When our kids come home from wherever they are, they come here.

"Home" is here, so I am too. For now. As I have learned too well, nothing is permanent.

Chicago is also a big part of that. On Tuesday, May 14, 2019, I fulfilled my dream of having a public piece of art in Amy's memory installed in a place called Grandmother's Garden in Lincoln Park, our family's old stomping ground. I had spent nearly two years navigating the bureaucracies of the City of Chicago and the Chicago Park District. My kids and I all went to school near Lincoln Park, and it's a neighborhood where Amy spent many hours in local cafés.

With the help of Chicago artist Susan Giles; a Chicago-based design and production studio called Space Haus; my friend and general contractor Jeff; a structural engineer; the Chicago Park District; and a committee overseeing public art installations in local parks, and with the blessings of Chicago mayor Rahm Emanuel, a nine-foot-tall yellow umbrella now stands. The glass was hand-painted and manufactured in Germany and decorated with photographs the artist took of flowers that grow in Lincoln Park.

And last but certainly not least, the word *more* appears on the umbrella panels, positioned in such a way that when the sun shines at different times of the day, that same word is reflected on the ground. "More" was the first word Amy spoke in this life, and I can't think of a more perfect word for her to leave behind.

The day before this tribute to her, this celebration of her, was installed, I sat by myself in the park at sunset, silently admiring it, lost in thoughts of how much Amy would have loved it. My tears flowed, but my heart was so full.

Every square inch of my house and this great city makes me think of Amy. Honestly, though, what doesn't? Why fight it, when there are reminders of her everywhere, from a random bag of potato chips, to a corkscrew that was once a shadow puppet, to an exit sign that should read "excite," to a display of unique buttons that could make a great brooch, to the mail that still comes in response to Amy's column, and to some of the work I have put out in the universe since then?

I have come to a place where I have a deeper appreciation for what I had with Amy. I have made peace with the reminders I see about Amy. I have the realization now that I am one of the fortunate ones to have loved so deeply *and* to have experienced grief in such a profound way. It means to me that I was one of the lucky ones, to have cared and loved so much—why else would I have such intense reactions to my loss?

So I do not mind reminders of my past. In fact, I want more. When I go back to "You May Want to Marry My Husband," I now realize that Amy must have known what would happen to me if her piece was published in the Modern Love column. It meant that I would be the center of some significant attention.

She knew me better than any human being ever has, so maybe more of Amy means more is also where I am going.

Acknowledgments

I have many people to thank for helping me to the place where I can form these words now.

I want to thank Amy Krouse Rosenthal. If you got this far, you have read the body of this text, so I do not feel the need to expound too much more on this recognition. Just know that there are many spaces in between all of these thoughts that Amy has given me. In her life *and* in her death, Amy gave me so much. She knew how to appreciate the "crevices of life" as she described in one of her TEDx talks. She has indelibly taught me to welcome those small moments. And boy, do I appreciate them now. Thank you, Amy.

Justin, Miles, and Paris. I acknowledge you. I listen to you. I hear you. I respect you. I love you always. Thank you for reading this book prior to its publication. You honestly helped me, even with small comments, to make it better. We have many memories to make together and I look forward to every minute.

To all of the Krouses, Rosenthals, Liefs, Kaufmanns, and Froelich-Saltzmans, and Flavia. You are my world. I appreciate all of you beyond comprehension—all you have given me and the kids these past few years. Huge love, a warm embrace, acceptance, support, space, conversation, and understanding.

Thank you to my editor, Matt Harper. I mean, how much would Amy have loved the fact that my editor at HarperCollins is named Matt Harper? Matt, you plainly and simply made this book better every step of the editing process. Your manner and method of encouraging while also advising me on the path forward was a perfect blend. You have always been sensitive to the deeply personal story I have conveyed here, so thank you for that. Thank you, Jonathan Burnham, for believing that I had a story to tell. Lisa Sharkey, thank you for putting up with me through every phase of this process, knowing that I was a novice. Your guidance, sage words, and support got me through and I am so grateful. The entire Harper team made this possible— thanks for being such champions of this work and for your dedication and professionalism.

To my early readers: Claire, Ann, Ruby, Amy Rennert, Justin, Miles, and Paris. Without your words of wisdom, I would not have been able to release this book out into the universe. Each of you gave me such solid, spot-on, and sagacious advice. I am forever indebted to each of you. And to Lindsay, for helping me shape my story, I have deep gratitude.

To my friends. How did you know just exactly how to act, what to say, and when I needed you? Thanks to each and every one of you. My Heal Jason Tour brothers: Michael, Mark, Sevem, Cary, My Friend George, Dave, Jeff, and my Specter mates as well. Special shout-out to Michael for coming up with the *Heal Jason Tour* title. More important, thanks to your partners and wives for letting you let loose with me.

Thank you to my office mates who were really there for me

when I just could not tackle the day-to-day: Larry, Tim, Nick, Nancy, Dan, C.J., and Jessica.

My brother, Rob. There are not many people I could live with in a tiny space in the middle of the desert with no shower sporting a tutu on a Tuesday. Thank you for exposing me to the playa world and for your friendship. Gratitude and love to my Mystic and Alchemist families as well.

For getting my body and mind to a place where I felt ready to embrace my blank page: Aileen, the princess of Pilates; Ron, for kicking my butt; Sarah, for sculpting me into shape; Sam Harris, though I do not know you, I feel as though I do as I hear your voice daily in my meditation practice; and Claire, for being *the* best yoga instructor I have ever practiced with by far. Thank you to my therapist for listening to and guiding me through this time in my life.

Kelly, I had no idea what I was getting into with the TED talk, but you had a vision. Thank you for pushing me out of my comfort zone and giving me the opportunity to step into that iconic red circle.

Thank you, Sheryl and Katie, for sharing your stories of loss and hope with me. The conversations, emails, and texts we shared have supported me abundantly. I am trying to pay it forward following your leads.

Thank you, Wendy and Jimmy, for friendship, for your amazing family, and for sharing Montana with me at such a poignant time.

Thank you, Daniel Jones and Brian Rea, for making my Modern Love column worthy of sharing with the universe. You both helped me convey my message in an impactful and beautiful way.

Amy Rosenberg. You have encouraged me not to suck for a

couple of years now and I hope this holds up to that scrutiny. Honestly, though, I appreciate your love and support and your guidance through all things life has brought me in the recent past. The other Amy R., Amy Rennert, I am honestly the luckiest man to have you by my side. Thanks for helping me navigate my way through the film and literary mazes. I am grateful too that we have gotten closer and can share the intimate moments that life brings us. Betsy, thank you so much for all you do with our foundation and giving me the freedom to spend time writing this book.

Brooke Hummer Mower, you are a creative force. You are also a dear friend and I consider you a partner in this end product that you are currently holding in your hands. I can't say enough about how you helped me see my creative vision come to life with the images contained in these pages (and for making me look half decent too).

To all of you who have reached out to me—thank you for connecting. I know I did not reach out to each and every one of you, but here in these pages I have tried to show my appreciation. Please know that our shared story will continue to be told.

To my hazel-eyed twin for filling my blank page with joy and happiness—thank you.

About the Author

Jason B. Rosenthal is the number one *New York Times* bestselling author of *Dear Boy*, cowritten with his daughter, Paris. He is the board chair of the Amy Krouse Rosenthal Foundation, which supports both childhood literacy and research in early detection of ovarian cancer. A lawyer, public speaker, and devoted father of three, he is passionate about helping others find ways to fill their blank spaces as he continues to fill his own. Jason resides in Chicago, a city he is proud to call home.

For more information about the Amy Krouse Rosenthal Foundation, please visit: amykrouserosenthalfoundation.org.